MONTH-BY-MONTH
PHONICS
FOR SECOND GRADE
SYSTEMATIC, MULTILEVEL INSTRUCTION

by
Dorothy P. Hall
and
Patricia M. Cunningham

Project Coordinator
Joyce Kohfeldt
I.E.S.S., Kernersville, NC

Editor
Wolfgang Hoelscher

Illustrators
Gene Shanks
Pam Thayer

DEDICATION

This book is dedicated to second-grade teachers everywhere and especially those teachers who have shared ideas with us and whose superb teaching inspired the writing of this book. There are many whose names we have forgotten—or, in some cases, never knew. But we learned from the questions they posed and the solutions they offered. Particular thanks goes to the following teachers with whom we have worked most closely during the past ten years:

Kellie Alston

Yolander Bailey

Denise Boger

Rusty Dahler

Marie Daniel

Margaret Defee

Glenda Greene

Cindy Harper

Christine Joyner

Janet Leonard

Athlene Lockhart

Susie Marion

Sonja Patrick

Heidi Reckord

Adrienne Reynolds

Linda Wigley

ISBN 0-88724-492-0

TABLE OF CONTENTS

INTRODUCTION

Phonics is the current "hot topic." Everyone is talking about phonics and everyone has an opinion about what should be taught, when, and how. Phonics IS an important part of beginning reading instruction. But phonics is not all that matters. In fact, children who come to school with limited reading experiences and who are taught in a "phonics first, phonics only" approach often get the idea that reading is "sounding out words!" You do have to figure out words but reading is not figuring out words and "sounding good." Figuring out words is the means to the end of understanding, learning from, thinking about, and enjoying stories and print.

It seems foolish as we approach a new millennium to have to point out this basic fact. Decades of research support the idea that children need phonics, but children who are only taught phonics until they "get it" are not suddenly transformed into eager, meaning-seeking, strategic readers. Good readers do know phonics and they use phonics to figure out some words. But good readers also recognize the most frequent words instantly as sight words. They use context to check what they are reading and if the words they have figured out make sense.

Teaching all our children to read is essential and can be done. But it will never happen with a "just teach 'em phonics" curriculum. Children do not all learn in the same way. Some children do learn to read by reading. Other children learn to read through writing. Some children learn sight words very quickly and know words forever after just reading them once or twice. These fast word learners don't do much decoding while they read because they don't need to!

The word "balance" is currently in danger of extinction from overuse. But the concept of balance is and will remain a critically important idea. To us, balance in reading instruction is like a balanced diet. We make sure that children eat from the different food groups because each group of foods is important to growth. We decide how much of each group should be included in a balanced diet and these amounts change as people grow older. We do not try to decide which group is best nor do we go through phases in which "experts" recommend that children eat only from one group!

To become good readers, children need a balanced reading diet. The "food groups" of balanced reading instruction are: Guided Reading, Self-Selected Reading, Writing and Working with Words. In numerous successful primary classrooms in which we have worked, teachers divide their language-arts time each day into four blocks of 30-40 minutes each. In Four-Blocks classrooms, children spend one-quarter of their time in Shared and Guided Reading of books and stories chosen and guided by the teacher. They spend another quarter of their time in Self-Selected Reading where they choose what they want to read. Another quarter of their time is spent in Writing. Another quarter is spent Working with Words, including sight words, phonics and spelling.

This book provides month-by month activities for one-quarter of a well-balanced reading diet—the Working With Words Block. When combined with the other essential components—Guided Reading, Self-Selected Reading and Writing—all children grow at their optimum rates.

Many years of working in Four-Blocks classrooms have convinced us that each of the four components is equally important and that, in spite of what comes in and out of fashion, children develop best as readers and writers when their daily instruction provides this balanced reading diet. We invite you to read the description of the Four-Blocks program at the end of this book and use your own experience with teaching and children to decide if you are satisfied with the balanced reading diet you are providing your second graders.

Finally, as you begin this book, **we would like you to think about the kind of phonics instruction you will find here. For a long time, the phonics debate centered on whether to teach using a synthetic or analytic approach. Synthetic approaches generally teach children to go letter-by-letter, assigning a pronunciation to each letter and then blending individual letters together. Analytic approaches teach rules (The _e_ on the end makes the vowel long.). Brain research, however, suggests that the brain is a pattern detector, not a rule applier, and that, while we look at single letters, we are not assigning them sounds; rather we are looking at clusters of letters and considering the letter patterns we know** (Adams, 1990).

When good readers first see a phonetically regular word such as **swoop** or **quest**, they immediately assign them a pronunciation. This happens so quickly that readers are often unaware that they have not seen the word before and that they had to "figure it out." **Successful decoding occurs when the brain recognizes a familiar spelling pattern. Swoop** and **quest** could be quickly decoded or spelled by using the similar known words, **loop, troop, best, west. This process of using other words with similar patterns to figure out the unfamiliar word is commonly called decoding by analogy** (Cunningham, 1995).

English is not a simple language to learn how to decode and spell. Many of the consonants and all of the vowels have a variety of sounds depending on the surrounding letters. Vowels do not have just short and long sounds. This can clearly be understood by looking at any sentence and thinking about what the vowels do in that sentence. In the previous sentence, for example, the following words contain the vowel **o**:

understood, looking, about, vowels, do

None of these **o**'s represent the short or long sound of **o**. In the same sentence, the following words contain the vowel **e**:

clearly, be, understood, sentence, vowels

The **e** in the word **be** represents the long **e** sound and two of the three **e**'s in the sentence represent the short sound of **e**. The **e** represents different sounds, not short or long in **clearly, understood,** and **vowels. There is logic to the sounds represented by letters, including, vowels, in English, but the logic is in the pattern— not in simple "vowel rules."**

The phonics activities in this book are consistent with the brain research that supports the idea that decoding and spelling are not accomplished by sounding out words letter-by letter or by rules. Rather, children learn from the beginning how to use patterns in words they know to decode and spell hundreds of other words. In addition to phonics patterns, the book provides activities to help children develop a store of instant words—high-frequency words they can instantly decode and spell. Activities are also included to help readers learn the important strategy of cross checking—checking a word they have figured out to be sure it makes sense. We hope you find these activities a healthy and tasty addition to the balanced reading diet you are providing your second-grade readers and writers.

References

Adams, M. J. (1990). *Beginning to Read: Thinking and Learning about Print.* Cambridge, MA: MIT Press.

Cunningham, P. M. (1995). *Phonics They Use: Words For Reading and Writing, 2nd Ed.* NY: HarperCollins.

It's the first day of second grade! Last year's little first graders are now "big" second graders. Students who were successful at learning to read and write in first grade are anxious to get back to school and learn some more! They have had a taste of success and they like it. They almost demand that their second grade teacher continue this exciting literacy journey. Other students are just beginning to understand how this thing called reading works. If they have been fortunate, they have had a kindergarten and first-grade teacher who shared their love of good books and good stories, and these children are still excited about learning to read. **Regardless, it is not too late to help second graders and to watch them grow in both size and knowledge.**

It is not where these children are on their literacy journey that matters but that each child makes progress every year! There is no telling how much seven-year-olds can learn in a year when they feel good about themselves and are receiving good instruction that makes sense to them. We have watched many students whom we were worried about in first grade develop into good solid students in second grade. We have learned it is never too late to learn to read and write if children think they can! Your second graders have had some instruction in learning how to read and write previously, but watch out—summer is over and they are ready for more!

MONTH AT A GLANCE

By the end of the first 4-6 weeks, you will have reviewed the following:

- Concepts of print (checklist)
- Phonemic awareness
- Using students names to make letter, sound, and word observations
- Beginning letter sounds
- Rhyming words
- Key names for consonants
- Segmenting words into sounds
- Vowel sounds

You will also have introduced:

- Alphabet books and a picture dictionary to explore beginning sounds for beginning letter(s)
- A *Word Wall* on which is displayed many high-frequency words
- *Rounding up the Rhymes* as a way to focus on spelling patterns
- *Guess the Covered Word* as a way to cross-check using context, word length, and phonics clues

In this chapter, we will describe some **activities for the first 4-6 weeks of second grade that will help you see where your students are in their word knowledge—what they know about words and how they work.** These activities will also help students develop critical concepts they need when reading (decoding) and writing (encoding) while simultaneously convincing all the children that they are becoming readers and writers. Now, we know that our use of the word **all** has most of you shaking your heads and wondering if we have seen the second-grade classes in your school! While we haven't seen all the second-grade classes there are, we have seen enough to know what you are worrying about. **In most classrooms there are some children who come to second grade reading quite well, other children who can read but have more to learn, and still other children who are just at the emergent stage.** What can you do during the first 4-6 weeks of school that will meet the needs of this wide range of entering literacy levels found in almost every second-grade class? Can we review with the class and assess students' word knowledge while teaching those who haven't learned important print concepts yet? We will try to answer these questions in this chapter. **Children come to us at different literacy levels and they must sense that they are making progress if their eagerness and excitement is to sustain them through the hard work of learning to read.**

INFORMAL ASSESSMENT

In second grade, teachers begin the year by informally assessing students as they read and write. Teachers often want to know what these new students know and what they will have to teach this year. Because there is such a wide variety in what children know and can do at this time of year, teachers often begin by looking at those concepts needed to be successful in early reading and writing. Some important concepts to look for early in second grade are:

Print Concepts

Print is what you read and write. Print includes all the funny little marks—letters, punctuation, space between words and paragraphs—which translate into familiar spoken language. In English, we read across the page in a left to right fashion. When we finish a line, we make a return sweep and start all over again. If there are sentences at the top of a page and a picture in the middle and more sentences at the bottom, we read the top first and then the bottom. We start at the front of the book and go towards the back.

In addition to learning how to move our eyes to follow the print, young children **must also learn the "jargon" of print.** Jargon refers to all the words we use to talk about reading and writing and includes terms such as **word, letter, sentence,** and **sound.** We use this jargon constantly as we try to teach children how to read:

"Look at the **first word** in the **sentence**. How does that **word** begin? What letter makes that **sound**?"

Using some jargon is essential to talking with children about reading and writing, but children who don't come from rich literacy backgrounds are often hopelessly confused by this jargon in the early grades. Most second-grade students have a grasp of this jargon, but some have missed instruction taught previously because they did not understand the jargon and could not take advantage of the instruction at that time.

Although most second graders understand these concepts, for those who do not it is helpful to have a checklist with the names of these students on it. Many teachers use a checklist (a reproducible checklist can be found on page 147) that includes:

Concepts of Print Checklist	Tom	Sue	Bob
• Starts on left.	✔	✔	✔
• Goes left to right.	✔		✔
• Makes return sweep to next line.	✔		✔
• Matches words by pointing to each as reading.	✔	✔	✔
• Can point to just one word.	✔	✔	✔
• Can point to the first word and the last word.	✔		✔
• Can point to just one letter.	✔	✔	✔
• Can point to the first letter and the last letter.	✔	✔	✔

Teachers use the checklist as children are reading in a shared reading format with big books or during a mini-lesson when they model writing and ask the children to help them (shared writing). The teacher asks the children, who still do not have a grasp of these concepts, to point to what they are reading or to show them where they should write. She also asks them if they can show just one word, point to the first and last word, show just one letter, point to the first and last letters of a word. If they are successful, she puts a check in the column showing what they have demonstrated. **When a child has several checks in a column, the teacher can assume this child has an understanding of the concept and doesn't need to look for this concept anymore. When children demonstrate that they understand all of these concepts, the teacher draws a line through their names and then focuses the instruction and assessment on children who have not yet demonstrated these concepts.** In second grade, this may not take a long time and is well worth the effort for those who have not yet mastered these concepts. Knowing which children need a little extra nudge allows the teacher to give this help to those who need it when reading and writing along with everyone else in the classroom.

Phonemic Awareness

Phonemic awareness is the ability to manipulate sounds. Phonemic awareness develops through a series of stages during which children first become aware that language is made up of individual sounds, that words are made up of syllables, and that syllables are made up of phonemes. Children develop phonemic awareness as a result of exposure to oral and written language. Nursery rhymes, chants, and Dr. Seuss books usually play a large role in this development before school starts. Once in school, young children continue to listen to and then read stories; they also hear rhymes and rhyming words. They use what they have learned about letters and sounds when they read and write. These activities help young children see that words are made up of sounds and that sounds can be changed to make different words. Only when children realize that words can be changed and how changing a sound changes a word are they able to profit from instruction in letter-sound relationships or phonics.

Letter Names and Sounds

Most second graders have learned the letter names and can recognize all 26 letters in both upper- and lowercase. For those children we are still not sure of, **we assess each child's knowledge of letter names and sounds by giving them a sheet of paper on which the letters are listed in random order and ask the child to point to all the letters he knows. For the letters he doesn't know we ask: "Can you tell me what sound this letter makes?"** We note the response with "**S**" if he knows the **sound**. If he does not have the correct sound for the letter then we ask: "Do you know any words that begin with this letter?" We indicate with a "**W**" for **word** any letters the child didn't give us names or sounds but for which he has a word association.

Word Learning

Most second-grade children who have had reading and writing experiences have learned some words. **To assess their reading ability you may want to listen to each child read a book of their choice (or your choice). A good time to do this is during Self-Selected Reading time.** Have several easy and a few difficult first-grade books available. In second grade, one book for reading does not "fit" all. Other teachers have been trained in running records (Clay, 1993) or in giving Informal Reading Inventories (Johns, 1994) and carry out their assessment in this fashion. Some teachers, whose students have had a Word Wall in first grade, have the children read words from the first grade Word Wall list (Cunningham & Hall, 1997; Cunningham, Hall, & Sigmon, 1998). The expectation is not that everyone knows all the words (although some children will be able to do this), but everyone has learned some words and is adding to this store of words. **Most second graders' reading is measurable, and they are better at reading the words than they are at spelling them in second grade.**

Once you know your students, you will see that literacy comes easier for some than others. What you want to do is see what students know so that you can begin to help those that are behind their peers while furthering the literacy journey of the others. **Those second graders who do not have a strong sense of how words work need to focus their attention on letter names and sounds. Children who have phonemic awareness can tell you when words begin with the same sound. When they have learned something about phonics they can tell you what letter makes that sound.** What follows are several ways to get acquainted with your students while helping other students develop or improve their phonemic awareness and letter-sound relationships.

HOW GETTING TO KNOW YOU IS MULTILEVEL

We use many multilevel activities at the beginning of the year to introduce the children to each other and to find out what these new second graders know about words. **A multilevel activity is one where there are multiple things to be learned and multiple ways for children to move forward.** During the first weeks of school we want to get to know our children and review (or teach) some of the concepts taught previously. Names are the perfect way to accomplish both goals. Second graders are interested in themselves and their friends! Teachers may choose from these activities. What you choose depends on your class. Some of you will choose one or two activities and feel good about your class. Other teachers will have to do more.

Name Cheers

10 min.

Select five children each day to cheer for. Let their names be the first on your *Word Wall*. (More information about the *Word Wall* can be found on page 16.) Have each child come up and lead a name cheer, pointing to each letter in the name and saying, "Give me an **S**. Give me an **h**. Give me an **a**, and so on. Finish each name cheer by "chanting" all the letters in the name and shouting the child's name. (Think of a basketball game to get the routine here.) **Children learn letter names quickly when they associate them with the names of their friends and have cheered for them in a rhythmic fashion.** Let them write these five names, one at a time after the chanting and cheering, on a half sheet of writing paper. The children who know the letter names and the names of their classmates are practicing handwriting; this skill also needs to be reviewed at the beginning of the year and practiced daily throughout the year. In this way, you can accomplish two goals at once!

Letter Sorts

10 min.

Use large index cards or pieces of sentence strips with the students' names written on them. Point to one of the alphabet letters and have everyone who has that letter anywhere in their name come down. Count to see how many names have that letter. Next have these children divide themselves into first letter, last letter, or somewhere in between and count again. Have the children say each name—stretching out the letters to hear the sound. Decide if the letter has its "usual sound." The letter "s" has its usual sound in Samantha and Jason but not in Sharon.

Review Beginning Sounds

15 min.

So far, the activities described would be most appropriate in kindergarten or first grade (although many second graders—particularly dual-language children—could benefit greatly from these.) Second-grade teachers can also use the names of their children to review and teach important word concepts. With younger children, we generally use only first names, but, for your second-grade children, you may want to include last names. **Children need to understand that in English, letters have predictable sounds but that there may be more than one sound.** For this activity, **focus on the names that do not begin with vowels. First, sort the names according to the beginning letters—everything up to the first vowel. Then, have the children say the names and divide any whose beginning letters have different sounds.** Here are the names of the children whose names begin with "C" at the end of this sort:

Cathy	Cindy	Chad
Carol	Cybil	Charles
Conley		
Craig	Clark	
Cross	Clover	
Crump		

Once the names are sorted, help children see that sometimes, as in Craig, Cross, Crump, Clark and Clover, you "blend" the beginning letters together to figure out the word. Other times, such as in Chad and Charles, letter combinations such as **ch** have a special sound. **C**'s most common sound is the one at the beginning of Cathy, Carol, and Conley but **c** also has the **s** sound as it does in Cynthia and Cybil. Some children might have a simplistic notion that all beginning letters always have the same sound, and they look only at the first letter and guess the word. **This activity will allow you to review beginning sounds, including the importance of looking at all the letters up to the vowel.** Second-grade children do not consider this "boring and babyish" when it is their name and the names of their friends that they are thinking about.

Clap Syllables

The first way that children learn to pull apart words is into syllables. Say each student's name and have everyone clap the "beats" in that name as they say it with you. Help them to see that Jim and Pat are one beat names, Suzanne and Ryan have two beats, Ebony and Stephanie have three beats, and so on. Once students begin to understand, clap the beats and have all the students whose names have that number of beats stand up and say their names as they clap the beats with you.

Matching Beginning Sounds

Say a sound—not letter name—and have all the children whose names begin with that sound come forward. Stretch out the sound as you make it: "s-s-s-s-" for the **s** sound— Samantha, Susie, Steve and Cedric should all come forward. Have everyone stretch out the "s-s-s" as they say the names. If anyone points out that Cedric starts with a **c** or that Sharon starts with an **s**, explain that they are correct about the letters, but that now you are listening for sounds.

Hearing Rhyming Words

Call on students whose names have lots of rhyming words such as Bill, Pat, and Mike. Say a word that rhymes with one of the names and have students say the word along with the name of the rhyming child.

Segmenting Words into Sounds

Call students to line up by stretching out their names, emphasizing each letter. As each student lines up, have the class stretch out the name with you. **Can they hear and write the letters they hear at the beginning, middle, and end?**

Key Names for Consonants

20 min.

Using a roll of paper, make a banner on which you write all the consonant letters, common blends, consonant digraphs, ch, sh, th, wh, and c (s), g (j). Under each, write the name of every student in your classroom whose name starts with those beginning letters. For some beginning letters, you will not have examples. Brainstorm with your students the names of famous people that begin with that letter/sound and add a few famous names (Michael Jordan, Jeff Gordon, George Clooney, Ken Griffey, Jr., Hillary Clinton, etc.) so that every letter has at least one key name displayed with it.

It is important that your banner include the blends and digraphs because struggling readers often use only the very first letter when trying to decode or spell a word. When your students are reading or writing and they do not use the correct beginning sound, or use only one of the beginning letters, refer them to the key name banner.

b	bl	br	c	cl	cr	c(s)
Bobby		Brenda		Cliff		Cindy
Bill		Brian				

ch	ch(k)	d	dr	f	fl	fr	g
Charles		Dawn				Freddie	Gwen

Vowel Posters

(6 sessions—1 vowel per session)

20 min.

The vowels, of course, are harder and struggling students are usually hopelessly confused by all the jargon and rules they have not been able to learn. With struggling students, we avoid talking about whether a vowel is "long," "short," or "r-controlled." Rather we try to get them to use vowel sounds in words they know to figure out other words. In every class, the students' names will provide lots of examples for the common sounds for each vowel. Using poster board, make a chart for each vowel (including **y** when used as a vowel as in Cathy) on which you list all your students' names that contain that vowel. Highlight the vowel in each name for the vowel heading that column.

Read the names on the posters together, emphasizing the sound of the highlighted vowel. Cross through any vowels that are silent. When students are reading and having difficulty with decoding a word, direct their attention to the appropriate name saying something like, "Try the sound of **o** you hear in Donna."

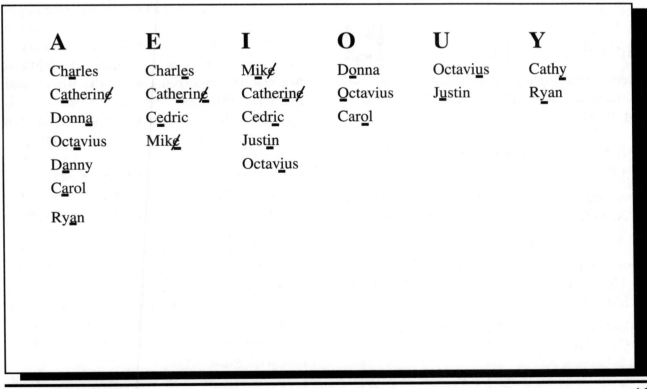

A	E	I	O	U	Y
Charles	Charles	Mike	Donna	Octavius	Cathy
Catherine	Catherine	Catherine	Octavius	Justin	Ryan
Donna	Cedric	Cedric	Carol		
Octavius	Mike	Justin			
Danny		Octavius			
Carol					
Ryan					

ALPHABET BOOKS AND A PICTURE DICTIONARY

There are also lots of wonderful alphabet books to read and enjoy. Many of these books fit nicely into your themes or units of study. Research shows that the simple books with not too many words on a page and pictures that most of the children recognize are the most helpful to children in building their letter-sound and letter-name knowledge. Once the book has been read and reread several times, children will enjoy reading it during their Self-Selected Reading time. **It is very important that children have time to choose and read books each day.** Simple alphabet books which have been read together are books that children can read on their own before they can read books with more text.

Alphabet Books

Here are a few alphabet books that meet our "not too many words, familiar pictures, kids love to read them" criteria:

A, My Name is Alice, by Jane Bayer. (Dial Books, 1990).

All Aboard ABC, by Doug Magee & Robert Newman. (Puffin Unicorn Books, 1990).

Animalia, by Graeme Base. (Puffin Books, 1996).

Annie, Bea, and Chi Chi Delores: A School Day Alphabet, by Donna Maurer. (Houghton Mifflin, 1996).

Basketball ABC: The NBA Alphabet, by Florence Cassen Mayer. (Harry N. Abrams, Inc., 1996).

A Fly in the Sky, by Kristin Pratt. (Dawn Publishing, 1996).

From Apple to Zipper, by Nora Cohen. (Aladdin Books, 1993).

From Letter to Letter, by Terri Sloat. (Puffin Unicorn Books, 1989).

A Jewish Holiday, by Malka Drucker. (Voyager Books, 1996).

The Monster Book of ABC Sounds, by Alan Snow. (Puffin Pied Piper Books, 1994).

NBA Action from A to Z, by James Preller. (Scholastic, 1997).

The Sweet and Sour Alphabet Book, by Langston Hughes. (Oxford University Press, 1997).

A Walk in the Rainforest, by Kristin Pratt. (Dawn Publishing, 1992).

Once you and the children have read several alphabet books, you might want to make picture dictionaries with your class. (Reproducible pages are at the back of the book on pages 151-154). The class works on a few letter pages every day, so that by the end of the first month of school, each child has a picture dictionary to use when writing. **The words can be recognized because the children choose the words and draw the pictures.** Brainstorm several words for each of the letter sounds; letting the children decide which one they want to put at the top of their page or section. All the **a** words go on one page. Then the **b** words will take two pages, with the second page divided in half—for **bl** words and **br** words. The letter **c** will take two pages both divided in half—one page for **c** and **c(s)**; the other page for **cl** words and **cr** words. Students use the *Word Wall* for high-frequency words and high-frequency spelling patterns as they write. The picture dictionary is a place to write other words that are not high-frequency words, but are words they want to spell correctly and need when writing.

Here are some ideas for each letter sound including the 50 "onsets" (letters and letter clusters that precede the first vowel):

A	alphabet, acorns, animals, adults	**Pl**	plants, plate, plastic, plow
B	books, bags, boys, boxes	**Pr**	pretend, practice, proud, pretzels
Bl	blinds, blouses, blink, blue	**Q**	questions, queen, quilt, quarter
Br	brown, brain, brother, broccoli	**R**	reading, red, robin, ride
C	computer, counters, caps	**S**	sink, six, seven, sun
C	city(s), celery, circus, circle	**Sc**	scale, scab, score, scarf
Ch	children, chowder, chalk, cherries	**Sh**	shoes, shop, shirt, shapes
Cl	class, closet, clothes, clown	**Sk**	skip, sky, skirt, ski
Cr	crowd, crayon, crab, cross	**Sl**	slow, sleep, slice, slide
D	desks, door, doctor, dish	**Sm**	smile, smell, smoke, smart
Dr	drawing, drain, dryer, drop	**Sn**	snack, snooze, sneakers, Snickers®
E	estimate, egg, eraser, easel	**Sp**	special, spy, spoon, sports
F	feet, fan, father, face	**St**	stories, stone, stem, stick
Fl	flag, fly, flip, flower	**Str**	stretch, street, strap, stream
Fr	friend, french fries, frog, frame	**Sw**	sweep, swim, sweets, swing
G	game, girl, goose, gate	**T**	teacher, table, tail, toaster
G	giant, giraffe, gym, general	**Th**	thumb, thimble, thirsty, think
Gl	glue, glass, glitter, globe	**Thr**	three, throne, throb, throat
Gr	graph, grain, grass, grape	**Tr**	triangle, tricks, train, trip
H	hamster, hat, house, hug	**Tw**	twins, twelve, twenty, twine
I	intercom, interview, ice, island	**U**	unicorn, umbrella, underwear
J	jump, jog, juice, jelly	**V**	violet, vines, vase, voting
K	keys, kangaroo, kite, kicking (the ball)	**W**	window, wall, watch, waffle
L	learning, lesson, lettuce, light	**Wh**	whistle, white, whopper, whale
M	making music, mother, mat, man	**Wr**	writing, wrist, wrong, wrinkle
N	names, nap, night, nickel	**X**	x-ing, x-ray
O	overhead, orange, octopus, obeying	**Y**	yelling (cheers), yellow, yawn, yarn
P	pencils, pants, paint, potato	**Z**	zippers, zebras, zero, Ziploc® (bags)

How Making a Picture Dictionary is Multilevel

When making the individual books with children, you are reviewing letters and the sounds that different letters and letter combinations make. For some children, this activity is important because they do not understand this concept yet. For other children, you are teaching them that certain letters make many sounds depending on the words they are in. The words for each letter and sound are more meaningful for children if they choose which words to write and draw. It is easier for children to remember that a word starts like "McDonald's®" if it is their word of choice rather than some word an adult or publisher has chosen. **A personal dictionary at any grade level is a multilevel activity because different children will enter different words depending on their word knowledge and their needs when writing.**

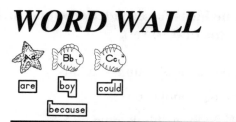

WORD WALL

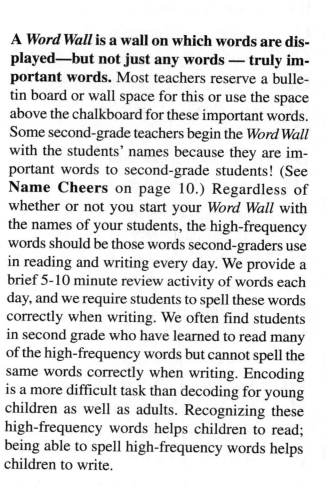

A *Word Wall* is a wall on which words are displayed—but not just any words — truly important words. Most teachers reserve a bulletin board or wall space for this or use the space above the chalkboard for these important words. Some second-grade teachers begin the *Word Wall* with the students' names because they are important words to second-grade students! (See **Name Cheers** on page 10.) Regardless of whether or not you start your *Word Wall* with the names of your students, the high-frequency words should be those words second-graders use in reading and writing every day. We provide a brief 5-10 minute review activity of words each day, and we require students to spell these words correctly when writing. We often find students in second grade who have learned to read many of the high-frequency words but cannot spell the same words correctly when writing. Encoding is a more difficult task than decoding for young children as well as adults. Recognizing these high-frequency words helps children to read; being able to spell high-frequency words helps children to write.

Adding Words to the *Word Wall*

Add five words to the wall each week. In second grade, we base our word selection more on what we observe in children's writing rather than on what words they have read during Guided Reading. **The emphasis is still on high-frequency words but we select those that are irregularly spelled, particularly those misspelled in their first-draft writing. Many second-grade teachers begin their *Word Walls* with the words *they*, *said*, *was*, *have*, and *because*, words most second graders can read but many cannot spell.** (We would not put high-frequency words that are easy to spell on a second grade *Word Wall* unless we had second graders who still couldn't spell **me**, **in**, **go**, etc.) These hard-to-spell high-frequency words are often on the first-grade *Word Wall* and then put back again on the second-grade *Word Wall*. In schools in which children have had a *Word Wall* in first grade, the students often know which words are hard for them to spell, and they ask to have these words put back on their second-grade *Word Wall*.

The *Word Wall* grows as the year goes on. Each week, the teacher writes the words on sheets of colored paper. It doesn't make any difference what colors you use, but try to avoid dark colors on which letters don't show up! The words need to be large enough to be seen from anywhere in the room. If two or more words begin with the same letter any week, be sure to use a different paper color for each of those words. After writing each word with a thick black permanent marker, cut around the outline of the letters to emphasize which letters go above and below the lines. Words are placed on the wall alphabetically by first letter, and the first words added are very different from one another. When confusing words are added, we put them on different colored paper from the words they are usually confused with.

Here is a partial sample of what your *Word Wall* might look like if you add students' names to the *Word Wall*. A commercial *Word Wall* for second grade is also available (CD-2503).

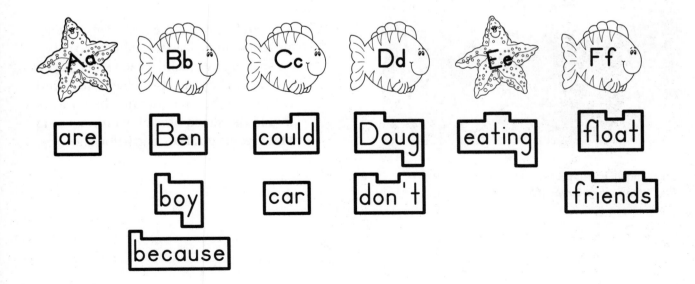

Most teachers add five new words each week and do at least one daily activity in which the children chant, cheer, and write the spelling of the words. The activity takes longer on the day that words are added because we take time to make sure that students associate meanings with the words, and we point out how the words are different from words with which they are often confused. Some teachers add the new words at the beginning of the week; others wait until the end of the week, keeping them separate for a while for all to see.

*Chart shown is from Carson-Dellosa's *Word Wall "Plus" for Second Grade* (CD-2503).

Daily *Word Wall* Practice

10 min.

1. Begin by giving each child a half sheet of handwriting paper on which they number from 1-5.

2. Call out five words, putting each word in a sentence. As the teacher calls out each word, the children locate the word on the wall and keep their eyes on it (**visual**). After you have said the word, have the children cheer for the word (or clap it or snap it). "S-A-I-D—said!" (**auditory rhythmic**).

3. Have each child write the word on the line beside the number 1 on his paper (**kinesthetic**). Write the word on the chalkboard or on the overhead projector as children write it on their papers. This will emphasize and verbalize the correct formation of the letters as the students follow you and write.

4. Repeat the procedure for the four remaining words.

5. After all five words are looked at, cheered for, and written, lead the children to check the spelling by touching each letter as you say them. They can also "shape" the word and look at their handwriting by drawing around the shape of each word, noticing which letters go above and below the lines.

This procedure of adding five new words a week continues. Practice the new words for a few days, and then spend the remaining days practicing words from previous weeks until there are approximately 120 words (not counting the children's names) on the *Word Wall*. Try to add your last words by April 15th (pay your taxes and put your last word on the *Word Wall*!). Spend the rest of the year reviewing and practicing the words your children still find the most difficult. These words are so important that we want to assure some "overlearning" so that most children will still be able to write them correctly after a long summer break away from school.

Selecting *Word Wall* Words

Besides the hard-to-spell high-frequency words, we try to include:

- an example word for letter combinations including **ch, sh, th, wh, qu, ph, wr, kn**

- the less common **c** (city) and **g** (gym) sounds

- the most common blends: **bl, br, cl, cr, dr, fl, fr, gr, pl, pr, sk, sl, sm, sn, sp, st, tr**

- the most common vowel patterns:

  a cr<u>a</u>sh, m<u>a</u>k<u>e</u>, r<u>ai</u>n, pl<u>ay</u>ed, c<u>ar</u>, s<u>aw</u>, c<u>augh</u>t

  e w<u>e</u>nt, <u>ea</u>t, gr<u>ee</u>n, sist<u>er</u>, n<u>ew</u>

  i <u>i</u>nto, r<u>i</u>de, r<u>igh</u>t, g<u>ir</u>l, th<u>ing</u>

  o n<u>o</u>t, th<u>ose</u>, fl<u>oa</u>t, <u>or</u>, <u>ou</u>tside, b<u>oy</u>, sh<u>oo</u>k, sch<u>oo</u>l, h<u>ow</u>, sl<u>ow</u>

  u b<u>u</u>g, <u>use</u>, h<u>ur</u>t

  y wh<u>y</u>, ver<u>y</u>

- the most commonly written contractions: **can't, didn't, don't, it's, that's, they're, won't**

- common homophones: **to/too/ two; there/their/they're; right/write; one/won; new/knew;**

- example words with **s**, **ed**, and **ing**

Here is a *Word Wall* list for Second Grade which includes everything just described in how the *Word Wall* is selected. (The boldfaced words are often used on a first-grade word wall, but it takes some children two years to learn to spell these words automatically every time they write.) Many teachers use a visual symbol beside or underline words with spelling patterns that help students spell lots of rhyming words. Common spelling patterns are underlined in the words below. This list also includes homophone clue words in parentheses to help students distinguish between words that sound the same but have different spellings and meanings. Each clue should be mounted on the *Word Wall* next to its corresponding homophone word.

Word Wall Words for Second Grade

about	friends	or	their
after	**girl**	other	**them**
again	green	our	th<u>en</u>
are	gym	<u>ou</u>tside	**there** (here)
beautiful	**have**	**people**	**they**
because	**here**	ph<u>one</u>	they're (they are)
before	**house**	pla<u>y</u>ed	**thing**
best	**how**	**pretty**	those
bl<u>ack</u>	hurt	**quit**	**to**
boy	**I**	**rain**	too (too late!)
brothers	into	really	tr<u>ip</u>
b<u>ug</u>	it's	**ride**	tr<u>uck</u>
can't	j<u>oke</u>	r<u>ight</u> (Wrong!)	two (2)
car	**jump**	**said**	use
caught	j<u>unk</u>	s<u>ale</u>	**very**
children	k<u>icked</u>	**saw**	wanted
city	kn<u>ew</u>	**sch<u>oo</u>l**	**was**
cl<u>ock</u>	l<u>ine</u>	sh<u>ook</u>	**w<u>en</u>t**
could	**little**	**sister**	were
cr<u>ash</u>	**made**	sk<u>ate</u>	**what**
crashes	m<u>ail</u>	sl<u>ow</u>	**wh<u>en</u>**
didn't	**make**	sm<u>all</u>	**where**
don't	many	sn<u>ap</u>	**who**
dr<u>ink</u>	m<u>ore</u>	sometimes	**why**
<u>eating</u>	n<u>ame</u>	sp<u>or</u>ts	**wi<u>ll</u>**
every	**new** (old)	st<u>op</u>	**with**
favorite	nice	**tell**	won
first	**not**	th<u>an</u>	**won't**
fl<u>oat</u>	**off**	th<u>ank</u>	wr<u>ite</u>
f<u>ound</u>	one (1)	that's	writing

How a *Word Wall* is Multilevel

A multilevel activity contains multiple things to be learned depending on what your students are ready to learn. *Word Wall* activities can meet the needs of a wide range of second-grade students because there are a variety of things to be learned in a short (10 minute) practice. Most second-grade students can read these words but cannot write or spell them. This daily *Word Wall* practice provides a second opportunity for some students who have not learned to read these high-frequency words in first grade. Other children learn to write or spell them correctly and are reminded to do so when they write in school everyday. The daily practice and the demand for the correct spelling of any *Word Wall* Word any time when writing will—eventually—help students replace the automatic incorrect spelling with an automatic correct spelling. You probably have some children who are already spelling all these words correctly. For them, **the daily practice is a time when they can work on their handwriting**—a skill many second graders have not perfected.

ROUNDING UP THE RHYMES

20 min.

Rounding Up the Rhymes is an easy activity for second grade-students, but it is fun! Often it is a necessary activity for students who don't understand the concept of rhyme yet. **This activity can follow up any story, book, or poem with lots of rhyming words. The first, and often the second, reading of anything should focus on meaning and enjoyment.** A wonderful book at the end of the summer is Mark Teagues' *How I Spent my Summer Vacation* (Crown Publishers, 1995). This is the story a boy tells the class about his summer vacation. He claims that his parents sent him to visit an aunt out West—where he was captured by cowboys and had many exciting adventures. What fun to listen to! What is real? What did Wallace make up and why? You will hear children adding their tall tales to the adventures of Wallace! Children love to make up a good story and tell what would have/could have happened to them.

The second or third reading of the book is an appropriate time to call the children's attention to the wonderful rhyming words. As you read each page or two again, encourage the children to listen for the rhymes as you say them. As children identify the rhyming words write them on index cards and put them in a pocket chart or write them on an overhead transparency.

"When summer began I headed out West.

My parents had told me I needed a rest."

When the children tell you that "West" and "rest" are the rhyming words you write those two words and then continue with the reading. **Some of the rhyming words will have the same spelling pattern (like *west* and *rest*) and some will not (like *crowd* and *loud*). When you are finished writing the rhyming pairs, have the children help you cross out or discard rhyming pairs without the same spelling pattern** (or remove them from the pocket chart and rip them up!) You will be left with the following pairs:

West	sit	say
rest	quit	okay
hat	tricks	land
that	sticks	cowhand
day	eat	sight
way	beat	fright
day	ground	display
say	around	away
	buckaroo	
	too	

Finally, remind the children that thinking of rhyming words can help them when they are reading or writing. Write a word that rhymes with the rounded-up rhymes and show it to the children. Have them put the new word next to the ones that will help them figure it out and then use the rounded-up rhymes to decode the word.

"What if you were reading and came to this word? (show **pound**) What words in the pocket chart would help you read this word? Yes, **ground** and **around** have the same spelling pattern and rhyme. Let's see . . . gr—**ound**, p—**ound**. That word is **pound**. They wanted a **pound** of meat."

Next, say a word they might need to write—but do not show it.

"What if you were writing and wanted to write the word **treat**, what words would help you to write the word **treat** correctly. That's right, **eat** and **beat** can help you write the word **treat**. **T-r**—and then the same spelling pattern '**e-a-t**' and you have **treat**."

You may want to continue this for a few more words (flight, tray) especially if this is the first time you have *Rounded Up The Rhymes* and transferred to reading and writing new words. For example, **sight** and **fright** will help you with **flight**; **day** and **say** will help you with **tray**.

Any book or story with lots of rhymes is a good candidate for a *Rounding Up the Rhymes* lesson. Many teachers tie this activity in with an author study of Dr. Seuss.

Books to Use with *Rounding Up the Rhymes*

Golden Bear, by Ruth Young. (Scholastic, 1992).

House Mouse, Senate Mouse, by Peter & Cheryl Barnes. (Rosebud Books, 1996).

The Monster Book of ABC Sounds, by Alan Snow. (Puffin Pied Piper Books, 1994).

My Nose is a Hose, by Kent Salisbury. (McClanahan, 1997).

My Teacher, My Friend, by P.K. Hallinan. (Children's Press, 1989).*

One Fish, Two Fish, Red Fish, Blue Fish, by Dr. Seuss. (Random House, 1960).

One Less Fish, by Kim Michelle Toft and Allan Sheather. (Charlesbridge, 1998).

Puffins Climb, Penguins Rhyme, by Bruce McMillan. (Harcourt Brace, 1995).

This Is the Sea That Feeds Us, by Robert Baldwen. (Dawn, 1998).

Woodrow, the White House Mouse, by Peter & Cheryl Barnes. (Rosebud Books, 1995).

Zoo-Looking, by Mem Fox. (Mondo, 1996).

*Another good book for the beginning of the school year!

Rounding Up the Rhymes is enormously popular with the children. They all enjoy chiming in on the rereading of the book and telling you the words that rhyme. Most second graders find this an easy task—this was not always true in first grade!

How *Rounding Up the Rhymes* is Multilevel

Rounding Up the Rhymes is also a multilevel activity. Struggling readers and writers whose phonemic awareness is limited learn what rhymes are and how to distinguish them from beginning sounds. Other children, whose phonemic awareness is better developed, learn lots of spelling patterns and learn that rhyming words often share the same spelling pattern. Our most advanced readers and writers become proficient with the strategy of using words they know to decode and spell unknown words. This proficiency shows in their increased reading fluency and the more sophisticated nature of the invented spellings they write.

GUESS THE COVERED WORD

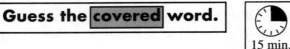

15 min.

When we read, we recognize most words immediately because we have seen and read them before. When we do see new words—words we have never encountered in reading before, we figure them out. **Many words can be figured out by thinking about what would make sense in a sentence and seeing if the consonants in the word match what you are thinking of. The ability to use the consonants in a word, along with the context is called cross checking and is an important decoding strategy. Children must learn to do two things simultaneously —think about what would make sense and think about letters and sounds. Most children would prefer to do one or the other, but not both. Thus, some children guess something that is sensible but ignore the letter sounds they know. Other children guess something that is close to the sounds but makes no sense in the sentence.**

In order to help children cross check meaning with sound:

1. **First have them guess with no letters showing.** The missing word is covered entirely with two self-adhesive notes, one for the beginning letters and one for the rest of the word. **There are generally many possibilities for a word that will fit the context.**

2. **Next, by pulling off the first self-adhesive note, the letters up to the vowel are revealed, thus limiting the possibilities.** You may have to make additional guesses if none of the possibilities are correct.

3. **Finally, show the whole word and help children confirm which guess makes sense and has the right letters.**

For each cross checking lesson, you will need to write sentences on the board or on chart paper, covering the word to be guessed with two self-adhesive notes, one of which covers all the first letters up to the vowel. **For the first lessons, we only cover words with a single beginning letter and place the unknown word at the end of the sentence. After these first lessons, we include words with letter combinations such as *sh*, *br*, and so on, and we place these words in various places in the sentence. When covering the words, tear your self-adhesive notes so that word length is visible. Word length plus beginning letters plus sense are powerful clues to the identity of an unknown word.**

Here are some sample sentences. Remember that using your children's names helps to keep them engaged!

Playing

Ryan likes to play **baseball**.

Michelle likes to play **tag**.

Refugio likes to play **football**.

Mrs. Daniel likes to play **cards**.

Jennifer likes to play with her **dog**.

Our Classroom

The **paper** is on a shelf.

Robert's **jacket** is in the closet.

Nancy sits next to **Billy**.

Paula's **lunchbox** is new.

The teacher has a big **desk**.

Pets

Maggie's favorite pet is her **hamster**.

Michael would like a **parrot**.

Kathy likes her **goldfish**.

Chuck likes his little **dachshund**.

Steve likes his new little **kitten**.

September

All the children are **happy** to be back in school.

They like to **shout** at recess.

Brittany has fun with her new **friends**.

Cindy likes to **stroll** around the yard.

Richard likes to run the **track**.

Ryan likes to play b[⬚⬚⬚⬚].

~~soccer~~   ~~football~~
~~sports~~   basketball
baseball

Michelle likes to play [⬚⬚].

ball   tennis
sports   tag

- The first thing you do is to show the children the sentences and tell them that they will read each sentence and guess what word you have covered up. Have students read the first sentence and guess what the covered word is.

- Next to the sentence, write each guess that makes sense (baseball, football, soccer, tennis, games). If a guess does not make sense, explain why but do not write this guess.

- When you have written several guesses, remove the paper that covers the first letter or letters (**b**). Erase any guesses which do not begin with this letter and ask if there are any more guesses which "make sense and start with a **b**."

- If there are more guesses, write these. Be sure all guesses both make sense and start correctly. Some children will begin guessing anything that begins with **b**. Respond with something like, "Bowling does begin with a **b**, but you don't play bowling, you bowl. Bowling does not make sense in this sentence."

- When you have written all guesses that make sense and begin correctly, uncover the word. See if the word you uncover is one the children guessed. If the children have the correct guess, praise their efforts. If not, say, "That was a tough one!" and go on to the next sentence.

Continue with each sentence going through the same steps:

1. Read the sentence and write three or four guesses which make sense.

2. Uncover the letters up to the vowel. Erase or draw a line through any guesses that don't begin with the correct letter.

3. Have students make more guesses which both make sense and begin with the correct letter or letters. Write these guesses. This is a "must" if they did not generate any guesses with the correct beginning sound.

4. Uncover the whole word and see if any of their guesses were correct.

26

How *Guess the Covered Word* is Multilevel

Guess the Covered Word is a multilevel activity because there are different things to be learned for different children. Struggling readers learn to use all the letters up to the vowel not just the beginning letter. When meeting an unknown word in text, they also learn to think, "What makes sense? What letter(s) does it begin with?" This is an important concept to learn in order to become a good reader. Average readers who know how to use context and phonics clues become more automatic at doing this. Because we use interesting words the accelerated readers learn more sight vocabulary and become even better at decoding.

APPLYING STRATEGIES WHEN READING AND WRITING

Some students read quite well without much help or guidance; other students need lots of easy reading so that they can become fluent. Easy, predictable books found in most second-grade classrooms are good for increasing fluency. So is rereading a familiar book. **Second-grade students need time to "practice" reading each day so that they may gain fluency, especially if they are still reading word by word.** No matter what the students' reading levels, comprehension demands that they have some speed and accuracy so that they can concentrate on the text's meaning rather than decoding the words. **Set aside some time each day so that your children can listen to you read and can read and reread their favorite stories and books.**

When writing, some students need to be reminded to use the *Word Wall*. Others need to be reminded to write words that are not on the *Word Wall* by saying them slowly and writing down the letter(s) for the sounds they hear. Having children think about letters and sounds when reading and writing helps children apply what they are learning during the Words Block to their daily reading and writing.

As you end September, we hope that most children have the desired level of phonemic awareness and letter/sound knowledge they need to be successful in second grade. We have done many activities with the students' names and you should know who is ready to use phonics and who is knowledgeable about beginning letters and sounds. For those students who have not yet mastered these concepts, it helps if you know who they are so you can continue to nudge them toward better understanding as we move into more advanced decoding and spelling activities.

This month, **we have started a *Word Wall* and let our children know that these are important words and must be spelled correctly**—and that is easy because you can look at the words on the wall when needed. We have also **had the children make their own picture dictionary.** (Maybe even one in a big book size for the teacher!) Now children who want to spell words (that are not high-frequency words) can spell them correctly because **they will have a personal dictionary to keep their own "special" words in. We have described two activities to help children develop and use their phonics knowledge—** *Guess the Covered Word* and *Rounding Up the Rhymes.* These two multilevel activities help children **learn how words work when they are reading and writing.** We know that for children to become good readers they need to read, **so we set some time aside every day to read to children and to let them read by themselves in self-selected materials.**

OCTOBER

October is here and autumn or fall is part of the conversation and learning in many primary classrooms. Fall is different in various parts of the country; in most places there is a change in the weather and, therefore, a change in the activities. Many areas continue the tradition of "celebrating" Halloween as a holiday at the end of the month. By this time in second grade, most classrooms have settled into a routine with some teacher-guided reading in basal readers or other books. Teachers also have a time each day to read aloud to the children. Children should also have time to practice new reading skills or strategies "on their own level" during a Self-Selected Reading time. Second-grade children also need a time each day to write. During this daily writing time, children write about whatever they want and then share it with the class on a weekly basis in an author's chair format. They also learn to take a piece from "sloppy copy" to "final draft"—but not every piece. **These three components—Guided Reading, Teacher Read-aloud/Self-Selected Reading, and Writing—form the core of a good balanced literacy program and should occupy the majority of the instructional time in any second-grade classroom. The other component—learning to read and spell high-frequency words and to decode and spell lots of less-frequent words—is the focus of this book.**

MONTH AT A GLANCE

By the end of October, you will have reviewed the following:

- Use of the *Word Wall* as a visual cue for spelling high-frequency words

- *On-the-Back* activities that help transfer *Word Wall* words to lots of other words by using the same spelling pattern in rhyming words

- *Changing a Hen to a Fox* to review beginning, middle (vowel), and ending sounds

- Coaching during independent and small group reading time

- *Making Words*—a three step, multilevel, hands-on activity:

  - Step 1—Making the Words to develop phonemic awareness and to figure out how words work

  - Step 2—Sorting the Words to help the brain become a pattern detector for beginning sounds, rhyming words and endings

  - Step 3—Transferring Words to extend the patterns to other words students will read and write

Working with Words Block

30 min.

The **Working with Words Block takes 30-35 minutes every day in second grade. The first 10 minutes should be spent practicing words on the** *Word Wall.* **That will leave you 20-25 minutes for another activity— a different activity can be done on different days.** You have learned two activities in the previous chapters— *Guess the Covered Word* and *Rounding up the Rhymes.* This month we will add two more— *Making Words* and *Changing a Hen to a Fox.* These activities help children develop word skills. These word skills are worthless, however, if children are not doing lots of reading and writing. In fact, only if there are lots of opportunities to apply their word skills in reading and writing will children get enough practice with words to become truly automatic and fluent in dealing with words.

Here are a few sources with rich descriptions of the other three components of a balanced reading program— **Guided Reading**, **Writing**, and **Self-Selected Reading**.

Classrooms That Work: They Can All Read and Write; 2nd Edition, by Patricia M. Cunningham and Richard L. Allington. (Longman, 1999).

The Four Blocks: A Framework for Reading and Writing in Classrooms that Work, by Pat Cunningham and Dottie Hall, Video available from IESS. (800-644-5280).

Implementing the Four-Blocks Literacy Model, by Cheryl Mahaffey Sigmon. (Carson-Dellosa, 1997).

*Invitations,** by Regie Routman. (Heinemann, 1995).

The Teacher's Guide to the Four Blocks, by Patricia M. Cunningham, Dorothy P. Hall, & Cheryl Sigmon. (Carson-Dellosa, Inc. 1998).

*Although Regie Routman does not mention "The Four Blocks" as such, the activities she writes about are all compatible with Four-Block activities.

As we move into October, our decoding and spelling focus is on learning more of the important high-frequency words that occur over and over in reading and writing. We do this with our *Word Wall* and add some *On the Back* activities to move the children forward in their word knowledge so that they use these words to help them write lots of other words. We continue *Guess the Covered Words* and *Rounding up the Rhymes* activities. We write some October (holiday) words in our alphabet books (picture dictionary) and add some *Making Words* lessons so that our seven-year-olds experience some hands-on phonics instruction. We review beginning, middle or vowel, and ending sounds by *"Changing a Hen to a Fox."* Learning about words can be fun!

WORD WALL

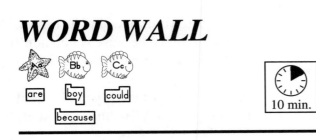

 10 min.

As outlined in the August/September chapter, **we continue to add five new words a week, usually choosing the words on the second-grade list which children misspell in their daily writing. If there is an interest in fall or Halloween words, remember your children will need them just this one month, so we don't use the** *Word Wall*—**which is the place for important words children need every day throughout the year. Put seasonal words on a piece of chart paper or a theme board or have students add them to their picture dictionaries.**

Doing a *Word Wall*

10 min.

Doing the *Word Wall* **is not the same thing as having a** *Word Wall*. **Having a** *Word Wall* **might mean putting all these words up somewhere in the room and telling students to use them. In our experience, struggling readers can't use them because they don't know them and don't know which is which! Doing a** *Word Wall* **means:**

1. Being selective and "stingy" about what words go up there, limiting the words to those really common words which children need a lot in writing.

2. Adding them gradually—five a week.

3. Making the words very accessible by putting them where everyone can see them, writing them in big black letters and using a variety of colors so that the constantly confused words (**for, from, that, them, they, this**, etc.) are on different colors.

4. Practicing the words by chanting and writing them because struggling readers are usually not good visual learners and can't just look at and remember words.

5. Doing a variety of review activities to provide enough practice so that the words are read and spelled instantly and automatically.

6. Making sure that *Word Wall* words are spelled correctly in any writing students do.

Teachers who "do" *Word Walls* rather than "have" *Word Walls* report all children writing these critical words correctly during daily writing activities. **Each day the Words Block begins with** *Word Wall* and by doing five *Word Wall* words. If teachers have time, we do an *On-the-Back* activity.

ON-THE-BACK ACTIVITIES
(SAME SPELLING PATTERN)

5 min.

The *On-the-Back* activity is so named because students do the activity on the backs of the handwriting papers used for the *Word Wall* words. **One of the activities we do is to choose a *Word Wall* word and use the spelling pattern to write other words.** You might present the activity by saying, "All of the words on the *Word Wall* are important words because we see them again and again when we read and need them when we write. Some words are also important because they help spell lots of other words." (For this example, we assume **went** is already on your *Word Wall*. If not, pick another word that will help your children spell lots of rhyming words.)

"**Went** is one of those helpful words. Today we are going to use it to spell other words. Write **went** on the back of your *Word Wall* paper then underline the spelling pattern—**ent**. Under the word **went** number your papers from 1-5.

1. The first word we are going to write is **tent**. What if you were writing about the **tent** you slept in on your vacation. The spelling pattern **ent** in **went** would help you write 't—**ent**'. Everyone write **tent**.

2. The second word we will write is **rent**. We had to move because we couldn't pay the **rent**. Write the word **rent**.

3. The next word is **sent**. My mother **sent** me to my room. Write the word **sent**.

4. The fourth word is a name, **Brent**. **Brent** is a new student in our class. Write the sounds you hear at the beginning of **Br—ent**, then the spelling pattern that follows.

5. The last word is **spent**. I **spent** all my money. Write the word **spent**."

Check the five rhyming words with your students letting them self-correct any words that need to be changed. Tell the students that these are words they should be able to spell correctly since **went** is on the *Word Wall* and the "ent" spelling pattern is there for them to look at when needed. Let them take their papers home and tell their parents they can spell these words. Parents like to know you are teaching their children to spell words correctly.

This *On-the-Back* rhyming activity can be done with any *Word Wall* word that has a spelling pattern that will help you spell lots of rhyming words. Be sure that your examples for each sentence sound like sentences your students might actually write. Doing this will achieve a maximum transfer to writing.

Some Words for *On-the-Back* Activities

For **clock** you can write **dock**, **lock**, **rock**, **sock**, and **shock**.

For **rain** you can write **pain**, **sprain**, **strain**, **train**, and **brain**.

For **car** you can write **bar**, **far**, **star**, **jar**, and **scar**.

For **stop** you can write **hop**, **chop**, **drop**, **shop**, and **top**.

For **thank** you can write **bank**, **blank**, **shrank**, **tank**, and **yank**.

For **boy** you can write **joy**, **Roy**, **soy**, **toy**, **Troy**, and **enjoy**.

For **ride** you can write **hide**, **wide**, **side**, **bride**, **glide**, and **slide**.

For **best** you can write **nest**, **rest**, **chest**, **vest**, and **west**.

For **jump** you can write **bump**, **dump**, **pump**, **plump**, and **thump**.

Each week when you introduce five new words, look and see which words have spelling patterns that can be used to make other words. Then, have your children turn over their papers and do the *On-the-Back* activity.

ROUNDING UP THE RHYMES

20 min.

Remember to be on the look out for text with lots of rhyming words when you are reading aloud to your children or when they are reading a selection during Guided Reading. A wonderful book to read to your students in October is Abby Levine's *This is the Pumpkin* (Albert Whitman & Co, 1997). **This story is written as a cumulative rhyme describing the activities of Max, his younger sister, and other children as they celebrate Halloween at school and "trick-or-treating" at home.** Children love this story about a day that is familiar to some children and not so familiar to others, depending on the local custom. The students like to share how they will celebrate this day at school and at home—if they will. **Once again the first reading is to listen to the story and enjoy the book.**

The second or third reading of the book is an appropriate time to call the children's attention to the wonderful rhyming words. As you read each page, **encourage the children to listen for the rhymes as you say them. As children identify the rhyming words write them on index cards and put them in a pocket chart or on an overhead transparency.**

"This is the costume, ghastly and **green**, that Max and his mom made for **Halloween**."

The children should tell you that "green" and "Halloween" are the rhyming words. Then, write those two words on index cards and put them in the pocket chart. Some teachers use the chalkboard, others use an overhead transparency. The important thing is that once they "hear" the rhymes, they can then "see" the rhyming words. Some of the rhyming words will have the same spelling pattern (like **green** and **Halloween**; **block** and **o'clock**) and some will not (like **street** and **treat**). When you are finished writing the rhyming pairs, it will look like this:

Notice how some of the rhyming pairs have the same spelling pattern and others do not. Have the children help you cross out or discard rhyming pairs that do not have the same spelling pattern. If you use a pocket chart, remove these index cards and rip them up! This really makes the impression that if words do have the same spelling pattern they are more helpful. If they don't have the same spelling pattern, they are not as useful. Remove words that do not have the same spelling pattern. These words remain:

~~green~~	~~block~~
~~Halloween~~	~~o'clock~~
~~west~~	~~parade~~
~~vest~~	~~lemonade~~
bright	stair
night	air
street	be
Treat	me
beds	eye
heads	sky

~~green~~	~~block~~
~~Halloween~~	~~o'clock~~
~~west~~	~~parade~~
~~vest~~	~~lemonade~~
bright	stair
night	air
~~be~~	
~~me~~	

Finally, remind the children that thinking of rhyming words can help them when they are reading or writing. Say something like:

"What if you are reading and come to this word?" (Write the word **between** on an index card; then show it to class—do not say it.) "What words in the pocket chart would help you read this word? Yes, **between**, **green**, and **Halloween** have the same spelling pattern and rhyme. Let's see...**be—tw—een**." (Model this thinking and separating of sounds so that children will understand what you do when you come to a word and you know the spelling pattern but not the word). "The word is **between**. He was sitting **between** his two friends."

"What if you were writing and wanted to write the word **light**, what words would help you to write the word **light** correctly? That's right, the spelling pattern in **bright** and **night** can help you write the word **light**. **L**— and then the same spelling pattern '**i-g-ht**' and you have the word **light**."

You may want to continue this for a few more words (chair, chest); especially if your second graders need more practice transferring these words to reading and writing.

Another book for this activity in October is Alan Snow's *The Monster Book of ABC Sounds* (Dial Books for Young Readers, 1991; Puffin Pied Piper, 1994). Monsters are fun to read about. Children like to pretend they're real! Since it is an alphabet book you can review letter/sounds or finish your picture dictionary with this book. After you read the story for enjoyment, you may want to stop and make a chart of the monster sounds in alphabetical order. Then, we round up the rhymes.

"The hide-and-seek game is about to **begin** . . .
The door is ajar and the rats go right **in**.
(This monster wasn't quite ready.)
Aaaaah!"

Have the children tell you the rhyming words on this page. Begin and **in** are the rhyming words. **We write them down so that the children can see the spelling patterns that are alike and then read the next two pages.**

"Bb   A monster pops out from behind the **door**

Cc   while three cunning rats sneak a look 'neath the **floor**."

Stop and have the children tell you the two rhyming words (**door** and **floor**) on these two pages. Continue through the book reading, identifying rhyming words, and writing those rhymes. When you are finished, these words will be left in your pocket chart, on the chart or on the transparency.

begin	door	o'clock
in	floor	shock
wet	feet	song
pet	eat	long
kicks	luck	mean
tricks	duck	seen
thirst	boast	great
first	most	late
be		
Z		

Next, we want to discard the words that do not have the same spelling patterns. We discard *feet/eat*, *mean/seen*, *boast/most*, *great/late*, and *be/Z*. These words remain:

begin	door	o'clock
in	floor	shock
wet	song	kicks
pet	long	tricks
luck	thirst	
duck	first	

"What if you were reading and came to the word **strong**? What two words would help you figure out how to read (say) that word? Right! The pattern in **song** and **long** will help you read **strong**. What if you were writing and wanted to write **stuck**, what spelling pattern would help you? That's right '**u-c-k**,' because **stuck** rhymes with **luck** and **duck**. Listen, stretch it out—**s-t**—**uck**—and write '**st**' then the '**uck**' spelling pattern."

Do this activity again using two more transfer words like **bricks** and **knock**.

"The word **bricks** uses the spelling pattern '**icks**' like in **kicks** and **tricks**. The word **knock** uses the spelling pattern '**ock**' like in **o'clock** and **sock**."

GUESS THE COVERED WORD

Guess the covered word.

15 min.

Some children never become really good at putting sounds together to decode words, but most words can be figured out by students if they look at the beginning letters, the length of the word, and if they think about what makes sense. Have you noticed your students saying, "That word couldn't be **peanut butter**. That is two words; besides, it's too short. It has to be a short word like **pear** or **pie**. This is the cross-checking ability that *Guess the Covered Word* helps children develop. You can do *Guess the Covered Words* for themes you are studying or books you are reading, too. **This month the word can appear in different parts of the sentence and can begin with two and three letter clusters—not just a one letter sound.**

Favorite Foods

Kevin likes to eat **cheese** sandwiches.

Billy likes to eat **pretzels** for a snack.

Fried **chicken** is Robert's favorite food.

Whitney likes **crackers**.

Suzanne likes **bread**.

Marie likes to eat chocolate **brownies**.

Halloween

The **children** went to a party in a van.

The **clothes** people wore were funny.

At the party someone had a **black** mask.

The **princess** had the best costume.

The **dragon** was the scariest.

After reading *The Monster Book of ABC Sounds* you can write sentences summarizing the book:

The monster was hiding behind a **small** door.

The monster liked to **play**.

One monster ate **bread**.

One monster was **thirsty**.

The monsters and the rats had a **great** time!

* *The Monster Book of ABC Sounds*, by Alan Snow. (Dial Books for Young Readers, 1991; Puffin Pied Piper, 1994).

October

The **leaves** are turning colors.

The nights are getting **longer**.

The days are getting **cooler**.

The **children** want Halloween to come.

They will dress in funny **clothes**.

They will go to a **party**.

MAKING WORDS

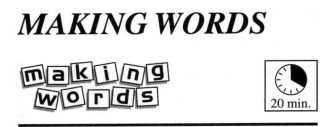

⏱ 20 min.

Making Words (Cunningham & Cunningham, 1992; Cunningham & Hall, 1994, 1997) **is an activity in which children are given some letters and use these letters to make words. They make little words and then bigger words until the final word is made. The final "secret" word always includes all the letters they have.** Children are always eager to figure out what word can be made from all the letters. Many teachers call this the "secret" or "mystery word." *Making Words* **is an active, hands-on, manipulative activity in which children learn how to look for patterns in words and how changing just one letter or where you put a letter changes the whole word. For most** *Making Words* **lessons, we use 6-8 letters including two vowels to make 12-15 words.** For the first lessons, however, it may be useful to use five letters including only one vowel to make 8-10 words. *Making Words* **takes a little bit of extra preparation time but will yield big results as children delight in their ability to create and manipulate words!**

Making Cards and Holders

The letter cards used in this activity can be easily made with tagboard or index cards, black and red markers, and scissors. Make a large set for yourself with all the letters of the alphabet or a set with just the letters you need for your lesson (i p r s t) on large index cards.

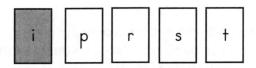

Use several pieces of white duplicator paper and write the letters (by hand or preferably on the computer). Divide one piece of paper into five columns from top to bottom, then make five equal rows going from left to right. Write a vowel in each of the rows, place it near the top of the box since the bottom of the box will end up in the "holder." Make 4 or 5 of each—"y" since it is a vowel when it makes the "e" or "i" sound. Capitals should be on one side of the paper, lowercase letters on the other side. Reproduce these on cherry (red) index paper.

a	e	i	o	u		U	O	I	E	A
a	e	i	o	u		U	O	I	E	A
a	e	i	o	u		U	O	I	E	A
a	e	i	o	u		U	O	I	E	A
e	y	y	y	o		O	Y	Y	Y	E

Divide the other two pieces of duplicator paper into boxes again. Make 2 or 3 of each of the consonants, except **q** and **x**—you usually do not have many words with these letters in them—on each sheet of paper until you have the whole alphabet written. Copy these master sheets for the consonants on white index paper—it is heavier and does not have to be laminated.

b	c	d	f	g
h	j	k	l	m
n	p	q	r	s
t	v	w	x	z
c	d	f	g	h

G	F	D	C	B
M	L	K	J	H
S	R	Q	P	N
Z	X	W	V	T
H	G	F	D	C

These letters can be used for a long time. The letter-boxes are then cut apart. Most teachers make a set for each child in the class to be used over and over again each time they do this activity. Some teachers put the letters in resealable plastic bags, one bag for each letter, and then take out only those 6-8 letters they need. Other teachers let each child have a set, and the children find the letters they will need for the lesson that day. We find that teachers vary on what they like to do and what they think works best.

Student word holders can be made by cutting file folders into 2" x 12" strips. For each holder, fold up about ¼" of a long side and tape the edges to make a pocket. The letter cards can be tucked into the shallow fold to make words in the holder.

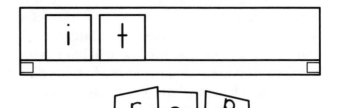

Preparing the Lesson

The teacher has decided that **trips** is the word that will end the lesson. She has pulled out (or made) the large letter cards for **trips**. She is brainstorming lots of little words that can be made from the letters in **trips**.

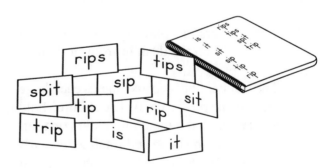

She decides which of the many words that she has brainstormed will make an easy and successful first lesson. She writes these words on large index cards (for **trips** she writes: **is, it, sit, sip, tip, rip, rips, tips/spit, trip, trips**). The letter and words cards are put in a small, brown envelope. On the outside of the envelope, she writes the words in the order the children will make them and the patterns she will have them sort for (beginning **s** and **r** sounds, rhyming patterns **ip** and **it**, and plural words are all possibilities). She may even write two or three good transfer words (**kit, skit, chip, ship**). Many second-grade workrooms have a communal box filled with hundreds of such brown envelopes. When a teacher finishes a lesson, she adds it to the box. Teachers can make up a new lesson or, in a pinch, use one already planned.

Teaching the Lesson

20 min.

The children are ready to make words.

1. Their letters are placed in front of their holders or on the desk in front of them.

2. The teacher holds up and names each large letter in the pocket chart. The children hold up and name the matching letters on their cards. Both the large and small letter cards have the uppercase letter on one side and the lowercase letter on the other side. The consonant letters are written in black and the vowel letters are in red. For these first lessons, the teacher and children show both the upper and lowercase letters and talk about the one red letter being the vowel.

3. They count the letters and decide that they have five—four consonants (black) and one vowel (red). The children and teacher are ready to begin *Making Words*.

4. Each child has the letters **i**, **p**, **r**, **s**, and **t** placed in front of the holder. These same letters are displayed on large cards in the pocket chart.

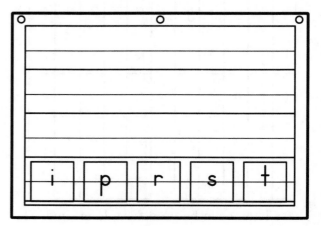

Step 1—Make

1. **The teacher tells the children that every word must have a vowel. Today they have only one vowel—the red *i*. They can put their *i* in the holder and work around it since every word will need it.** The teacher writes a **2** on the board and says,

"The first word I want you to make has just 2 letters—your **i** plus one more letter. The word is **is**. That is a word that most of us know. Everyone say **is**. Find the letter you need to spell **is**."

2. The teacher watches as many children put the **s** in their holder after the **i**. She then lets one child who has made **is** correctly in the little holder come up front and make it with the pocket chart letters.

    "Good, **i** and **s** spell **is**. Everyone check **is** in your holder and we are ready to make another word."

3. The teacher places the index card on which the word **is** has been written in the pocket chart. After each word is made with the big letters, the index card with that word is placed in the pocket chart. These index-card words will be sorted for patterns after all the words are made.

4. Next, the teacher has them make the word **it**, listening to what sound is different and trying to find the letter that makes that sound.

5. Then, the teacher writes a **3** on the board where the next column would be. The teacher tells them to leave **it** and add one letter to make the word **sit**.

    "I like to **sit** near my friend. Stretch out the beginning sound you hear in the word **sit**." Let the children who need to say the word out loud say **it** (children will do this almost automatically if they need to hear the sounds in a word before finding the correct letter). "Listen to the beginning sound in **sit**. Put that letter in your holder before **it**."

As children attempt to make each word, the teacher selects a child who has made that word correctly and sends that child to make the word with the large letters. Then, the teacher asks everyone to spell the word and make it before going to the next word. **It is very important for pacing and to keep the lesson moving—not to wait for everyone to make the word before it is made with the big letters-but everyone should make it once it is made with the big letters.**

6. Next, the teacher tells them to change one letter and spell **sip**. She gives them a sentence for the new word, "I like to **sip** my drink." She has everyone say **sip** stretching out the letters and listening for where they go. Some children in second grade still need to hear themselves making the sounds if they are going to transfer this ability to spelling words as they write. The teacher then finds someone with the word **sip** spelled correctly to make it with the big letters. She then puts the index card with the word **sip** in the pocket chart and asks the children to fix theirs if they need to.

7. The teacher and children continue to make the three-letter words—**tip** and **rip**. The teacher does not wait for everyone to have each word spelled correctly before sending someone to spell it with the big letters, but she does make sure it is spelled correctly before going to the next word. The index cards containing each word are placed in the pocket chart after each word is correctly made.

8. The teacher then writes a **4** on the board and shows the class **4** fingers. She says to the class, "Now we are going to make some four-letter words. If you add a letter to **rip** you can make **rips**." This will not be difficult for most children. "Next, change **rips** to **tips**, then change the letters around and you can make **spit**. We do not **spit** in school! Change the beginning two letters and make '**trip**.'"

9. **Now is the time to tell the children that when you plan the *Making Words* lesson, you always start with a "secret" word that can be made with all the letters. At the end of each lesson you will ask,**

"Has anyone figured out the secret word—one word we can make that uses all our letters?"

Tell them that some days they will be able to figure out the word and other days they won't, but that when they figure it out, they should keep it a secret until you ask the question.

"Take one minute and see if you can make a word that uses all the letters."

Give the children a minute to see if anyone can come up with the word—not likely if this is the very first lesson, but possible. **If anyone makes the word, send the child quickly to the pocket chart and have the child make the word. If not, tell them that the word is *trips*. Have a child go and make it with the big letters. Be sure to have everyone make the word *trips* correctly in their little letter folder.**

For the sorting phase, have the children close up the word **trips** in their holders and direct their attention to the words on index cards in the pocket chart. **Once the children get in the swing of *Making Words*, the making the words part should take no more than 10-15 minutes. That leaves five minutes at the end of each lesson for sorting into patterns and using these patterns to read and spell a few new words.** For the first several lessons, however, when the children are learning how to manipulate the letters and make words, making the words might take longer! After five or six lessons, however, you should have the pace down for the lesson so that the lesson is completed in the 15-20 minutes allotted to this activity. **Keep the pace of an average child who is making the words. Never wait for your slowest child to make the word—let them make it when one child comes up to make it with the big letters and the other children are checking. When it is fast-paced, even your shining stars stay actively involved, for they spell these words quickly.**

Step 2—Sort

The teacher and children are now going to sort the words for patterns, which at this time of the year consist of beginning letters and rhymes. Early in the year, the teacher directs the sort, but as the year goes on, the children should start to look for patterns. Today the teacher takes the word **sit** and asks,

1. "Who can go find another word that begins with the letter **s**?" A child goes to the pocket chart and places **sip**, under **sit**. The teacher and the class decide that they begin with the same letter and the same sound. The same procedure is used for **rip** and **rips**. Next, the teacher goes to the pocket chart and pulls out the word **it**.

2. "Now I need someone who can find two words that end in the letters **i** and **t**." A child places **sit** and **it**. Teacher and children pronounce the two words and decide that they are both spelled **it** and they both rhyme.

3. The same procedure is followed with **sip**, **tip**, and **trip**.

Step 3—Transfer

Finally, when all the rhyming words are sorted, the teacher says:

1. "When you are reading, you will see lots of words that end in **it**, or **ip**—you can figure them out on your own if you think about how words with the same vowel and ending letter usually rhyme. What if you were reading and came to these words?"

   The teacher writes the word **kit** and **chip** on index cards without pronouncing them or saying them out loud. Children put these words under the rhyming words and then use the rhyming words to figure them out.

2. "Thinking of a rhyming word can help you when you are writing too. What if you were writing and needed to figure out how to spell **skit** or **ship**?"

   The children decide that **skit** rhymes with **it** and **sit**. Then, **skit** is written on an index card and placed under **it** and **sit**. Next, **ship** is spelled and then placed under **tip**, **rip**, and **sip**.

(A blank Take Home Sheet for *Making Words* can be found on page 148.)

Making Words: More Easy Lessons

One of the most difficult decisions teachers make is when to move on to more difficult formats. Our observations tell us that some teachers move too fast, leaving a trail of struggling kids behind; others wanting everyone on board, never move! Of course, we must find some kind of middle ground—easier said than done!

Most *Making Words* lessons in second grade will have 6-8 letters, including two vowels. But children do need some practice with fewer letters and just one vowel so that they learn that there are vowels and what the vowels are. Later lessons will have silent letters and letter combinations such as "ch," "sh," etc., but, in the first lessons, children need to learn that if you "stretch out words, you can hear a lot of the letters." This understanding really moves them along in their ability to spell words while writing. At any rate, here are six more easy lessons for a total of seven lessons this month.

Secret word: acorns
Letters: a, o, c, n, r, s
Make: as, an, on, or, ran, can, car, cars, cans/scan, corn, acorns
Sort: c-, -an, plural words
Transfer: van/vans, pans, plans

Secret word: tracks
Letters: a, c, k, r, s, t
Make: as, at, sat, cat, car, rat, tar, tack, rack, sack, stack/tacks, racks, track, tracks
Sort: c-, t-, -at, -ar, -ack
Transfer: scat, flat, star, smack

Secret word: splash
Letters: a, h, l, p, s, s
Make: as, has, sap, lap, ash, sash, lash, laps/slap, slaps, slash, splash
Sort: s-, l-, sl-, -ap, -ash
Transfer: cash, crash, cap, trap

Secret word: pumpkin
Letters: i, u, k, m, n, p, p
Make: up, in, ink/kin, pin, pun, pup, pump, pink, mink, pumpkin
Sort: p-, -in, -ink
Transfer: win, twin, wink, stink

Secret word: rabbits
Letters: a, i, b, b, r, s, t
Make: at, sat, rat, bat, bar, tar, star, stir, stair, rabbits
Sort: b-, st-, -at, -ar
Transfer: that, flat, jar, scar

Secret word: ghost
Letters: o, g, h, s, t
Make: to, so, go, got, hot, hog, hogs, host/shot, ghost
Sort: g-, h-, -ot, -ost
Transfer: pot, rot, post, most

How *Making Words* is Multilevel

Making Words has become enormously popular with teachers and children. **Children love manipulating the letters, trying to figure out the secret word, and finding the patterns.** *Making Words* **works for children because (if your pacing is brisk!) they are all active, engaged, and successful!** Teachers like *Making Words* because the children do, of course, but also because **they can see all levels of children growing in their word knowledge. Every lesson begins with some short easy words, and as the words get harder, the teacher makes sure everyone has the word made correctly after it is made with the pocket chart letters.** In these early lessons, **some of our strugglers are still learning to identify letters and developing concepts such as first letter, last letter, beginning of word, end of word.** They are still developing their phonemic awareness and learning that sounds in words can be manipulated. *Making Words* lessons let them succeed and practice on whatever level they are on.

For most children who have never done this activity before second grade, *Making Words* is an activity through which **they are learning letter-sound relationships by stretching out words, hearing themselves making the sounds, and trying to match them to a limited set of letters.** Some children can do this quite easily; others cannot, but they will learn. **As they sort for beginning sounds and rhymes, they are beginning to understand how words work.**

Every second-grade class, however, contains **some children whose letter-sound knowledge when they start the year is way beyond simple beginning sounds and rhyming concepts.**

- These children are always eager to figure out the secret word. As they try to do this, they are working with concepts well beyond initial sound and rhyme.

- It is also for these children that at the end of every *Making Words* lesson—even the first one—the teacher shows them how the patterns in the words can help them figure out words in their reading and writing.

- Children enter second grade with all different levels of word knowledge. *Making Words* activities allow the whole range of children to make discoveries about words.

CHANGING A HEN TO A FOX

15 min.

Teachers want to know how much their students know about letter sounds. They watch them during *Making Words* but there is no number right or wrong recorded—and there shouldn't be! But sometimes teachers want to see how well their students do on paper. *Changing a Hen to a Fox* is one such activity. The teacher writes key words on the board:

cat	hen	pig	fox	bug

She asks them to say these words with her and calls the children's attention to the fact that they can hear the beginning, middle, and ending sounds in each of these words. Next she asks the children, "Can you change a hen into a fox?" She tells the children if they follow her directions and think about letters and sounds, they will be able do this.

"Write **hen**." This is already on the board so all can write **hen** easily by copying.

"Now, change **hen** to **pen**." (Give them a minute or less to do this—it is a one-letter change).

"Then, change **pen** to **pet**." (Give them a minute or less to do this).

"Can you change **pet** to **pit**?"

"Then, change **pit** to **sit**."

"Next, change **sit** to **six**."

"Then, change **six** to **fix**."

"Last, change **fix** to **fox**."

"If you have made these changes correctly, you have changed a **hen** to a **fox**!"

The students can correct their papers with the teacher. This activity will help you know what each student knows about beginning, ending, and vowel sounds.

Here are seven other lessons you can do with your class:

- pig, rig, rid, rib, rob, Bob, box, fox

- bug, dug, dig, pig, pin, pen, ten, hen

- pig, big, wig, win, fin, fit, fat, cat

- cat, bat, hat, rat, pat, pet, pen, hen

- fox, box, bop, top, mop, map, mat, cat

- bug, hug, dug, dig, big, bag, bat, cat

- cat, hat, rat, rag, bag, big, dig, pig

How *Changing a Hen to a Fox* is Multilevel

Changing a Hen to a Fox is really a review activity for beginning, middle (vowel), and ending sounds. The thought process that a student goes through in order to complete this activity is the multilevel part. Your more advanced readers and writers may know these words quickly. For these students, it is a time to recall and write words automatically using their word knowledge. Other students, who are not as far along in their word knowledge, learn to say the word slowly and listen for the sounds they hear. Then, they learn to write the letter that represents that sound. Your struggling students—and we all have some of these—are not only listening to the sounds but matching them to the sounds they hear in key words, then writing the letters on their papers. Children are different! What they need to be successful depends on what they know and the opportunities you give them. *Changing a Hen to a Fox* is a wonderful way to review letter sound knowledge. This activity also lets children, with a wide range of abilities, use what they know to write one-syllable words.

APPLYING STRATEGIES WHEN READING AND WRITING

Daily reading and writing continues along with the hope that the strategies taught during the Word Block will be used during the other three blocks. Some second-grade students know a lot more about letters, sounds, and spelling patterns than they actually use when they are reading and writing. The work you are doing with words and phonics is only useful if they use it while they are "really" reading and "really" writing. To learn something and not use it when needed is a waste of time!

Coaching During Reading

If you have children who read and stop when they come to a word they don't know, it will help to "coach" them. **Your instruction is more effective if you lead them through the steps to read a new word at the exact moment they encounter the word. Here are some suggestions when a student does not know a word:**

1. Put your finger on the word and say all the letters.

2. Use the letters and picture clues.

3. Try to pronounce the word by looking to see if it has a spelling pattern or rhyme that you know.

4. Keep your finger on the word and read the other words in the sentence to see if it makes sense.

5. If it doesn't make sense, go back to the word and think about what would make sense and have these parts.

A good reader looks at all the letters in a word he is trying to read. A child who is struggling with reading tends to look quickly at the word, and, if he doesn't instantly recognize it, he may stop and wait for someone to tell him the word or guess. Asking him to say all the letters forces him to look at all the letters. Sometimes, after saying all the letters, the child may say the word correctly!

By watching your children as they do the activities in the Words Block and observing and assessing the children one-on-one during the Self-Selected Reading and Writing Blocks, you will notice the progress the children are making.

- Some children do these tasks easily.

- Other children can do them but work hard to do so.

- Still other children need help to accomplish these tasks. It is these children we want to continue to focus on.

- We also want to be sure that the more advanced children are transferring this learning from the Words Block to reading and writing.

As the month is about to end with a scary holiday, teachers see that children are having fun, and it is a treat to teach phonics. Words are no longer tricking their students!

NOVEMBER

November is a good time to be thankful for the success your students are making in school this year. The classroom routines are well established and children are well on their way to learning more about how words work. Thanksgiving, one of our national holidays, is just around the corner. Many second-graders know about this holiday from kindergarten and first grade as well as the tradition of a Thanksgiving feast each year. Children like to talk about why the Pilgrims were thankful that first Thanksgiving in Plymouth, Massachusetts. Many of these seasonal words can be added to their Pictionaries. They will use these words this month but not again. That is why teachers have bulletin boards or theme boards—to capture some key ideas and words. These words can be used when writing about this topic.

Teachers also have several reasons to celebrate. Besides their family and friends, they are thankful for the young children in their classes who keep them busy, but who think they are wonderful. These same young children have many reasons why they are thankful. These reasons usually revolve around themselves—their food, their family, their home, their friends, and all the "things" they enjoy! Both teachers and parents are pleased that their children are learning to read and write. These are two blessings all of us should be thankful for!

MONTH AT A GLANCE

By the end of November, you will have reviewed the following:

- *On-the-Back* activities that help transfer *Word Wall* words to other words by using endings

- *Making Words* activities with seasonal words and more letters and vowels

- *Rounding Up the Rhymes* lessons which help students review beginning sounds and use the spelling patterns in rhyming words to spell lots of new words

- How lots of easy reading builds speed and fluency

WORD WALL

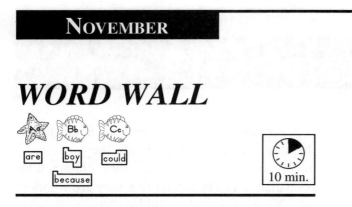

10 min.

ON-THE-BACK ACTIVITY (ENDINGS)

5 min.

In November, **we continue adding five words each week to the wall**, choosing the words from the second-grade high-frequency word list (see August/September, page 20). **They should be the words that many of your students are mis-spelling during their daily writing. Each week we continue calling out the new words for a few days, and then reviewing five words on the wall for two days.** Whether new or review words, **each day we have the children chant and cheer (clap or snap) for the words and then write them.** As the **teacher** writes them, **she models correct handwriting for all the letters in the words.** The children watch the teacher and form each letter in the word correctly. **Then, we have them self-correct their papers.**

Another activity you may want to introduce this month is how to spell *Word Wall* words with endings. When you finish your daily *Word Wall* practice, have the children turn over their *Word Wall* paper and do this activity on the back. ***On-the-Back* activities are designed to help children learn that some of the words on the wall can help them spell lots of other words.** The teacher, when beginning this activity, might say something like:

"All of the words we have on our *Word Wall* are important words because we see them over and over again in the books we read and they help us write. But some words are important in another way. If you know word endings some of the words on our wall will help you spell lots of other words that are longer but use the base (root) word, which is on the *Word Wall*. W<u>ant</u> is one of those helpful words." (Teacher circles or underlines **want** which was one of the five words called out to-day.) "We are going to practice using these *Word Wall* words when they have endings added on to them. Turn your paper over. Write the word **want**. Number from 1-5.

1. "The first word is **wants**. You might be writing about how your brother **wants** a dog. Let's say **wants** slowly and listen for the sound we hear at the end. Yes, **wants**, has an **s** added to the end. Everyone add **s** to **want**, and you have the word **wants**."

The *On-the-Back* lesson continues as the teacher gives them possible scenarios in which they would need to use endings to help them spell another word.

2. "What if you were writing about the football game and **wanted** your team to win? Say **wanted** slowly. What letters would you add to **want** to spell the word **wanted**? Yes, you add "e-d" to **want** and spell **wanted**. Everyone write **wanted** on the next line."

3. "What if you were writing about yourself and you are **wanting** to make friends with the new girl in the class. What would you add to **want** to write **wanting**. Yes, add "i-n-g" to **want** and you have spelled **wanting**. Write **wanting** on the third line on your paper."

After writing the word **want** with the different endings (s, ed, ing) on the back of your *Word Wall* paper, you will want to check them by reading and spelling the words together. Some other second-grade *Word Wall* words you can do this with are:

Sample *On-the-Back* Lessons with Endings

crash: crashes, crashing, crashed

drink: drinks, drinking, drinker

eat: eats, eating, eater

float: floats, floater, floating, floated

jump: jumps, jumper, jumping, jumped

kick: kicks, kicking, kicked, kicker

mail: mails, mailing, mailer, mailed

play: plays, player, playing, played

You now have two other activities to choose—rhyming words (words with the same spelling pattern) or endings on the back of the *Word Wall* paper. What you choose depends upon what words you are introducing or practicing each day.

ROUNDING UP THE RHYMES

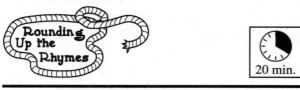

🕐 **20 min.**

A wonderful book to read to your students is David McPhail's *Those Can-Do Pigs* (Scholastic, 1996). **This book is written in rhyme and describes some "Can Do Pigs" that can do almost everything. As you read the book you will hear about the many feats of these bold and brave "super pigs." The first reading is to enjoy the book. The second reading may be to talk about, "Can this really happen?" The third reading of the book may be an appropriate time to call the children's attention to the wonderful rhyming words. As you read each page or two again, encourage the children to listen for the rhymes as you say them. As children identify the rhyming words, write them on index cards and put them in a pocket chart or on an overhead transparency.**

> "In the morning, bright and **early.**
> Can-Do Pigs are gruff and **surly**
> Till they've had their toast and **tea-**
> Then they're happy as can **be**"

The children should be able to tell you that "early" and "surly" along with "tea" and "be" are the rhyming words. Write those four words on index cards and put them in the pocket chart. Some teachers use the chalkboard; others use an overhead transparency. **The important thing is that they *hear* and *see* the rhyming words. Some of the rhyming words will have the same spelling pattern like out/snout and some will not like early/surly and tea/be.**

When you are finished writing the rhyming pairs, it will look like this:

early	tea	out
surly	be	snout
tie	ride	tire
bye	countryside	wire
roads	down	repairs
toads	around	chairs
new	anything	stick
glue	sing	brick
well	door	hot
fell	anymore	lot
lotion	pajamas	attacks
ocean	Bahamas	whacks
store	hiss	lie
boar	kiss	why
tree		
me		

This does not complete the book, but there are more than enough rhymes to round up. So don't feel you have to go through the whole book every time! Notice how some of the rhyming pairs have the same spelling pattern and others do not.

Have the children help you cross out or dis-card rhyming pairs that do not have the same spelling pattern. When you finish, you will have these pairs left:

out	ride	tire
snout	countryside	wire
roads	repairs	anything
toads	chairs	sing
stick	well	hot
brick	fell	lot
pajamas	attacks	hiss
Bahamas	whacks	kiss

Finally, remind the children that thinking of rhyming words can help them when they are reading or writing. This transfer step is an important part of the lesson. This shows that they can use what they know about words when they read and write.

"What if you were reading and came to this word?" (Show "**shout**," don't say it.) "What words in the pocket chart would help you read that word? Yes, **out** and **snout** have the same spelling pattern and rhyme. Let's see . . . **sh—out**." (Model this thinking and separating of sounds so that children will understand what you do when you come to a word and you know the spelling pattern but not the word.) "The word is **shout**. Connie had to **shout** to be heard."

"What if you were **writing** and wanted to write the word **slick**? What words would help you to write the word **slick** correctly? That's correct, the words **stick** and **brick** can help you write the word **slick**. **Sl**—and then the same spelling pattern "**ick**" and you have the word **slick**.

You may want to continue this for a few more words, especially if your second graders cannot easily transfer what they know about rhymes when they are reading and writing.

- tire/wire…fire

- stick/brick…flick

- attacks/whacks…cracks

- roads/toads…loads

GUESS THE COVERED WORD

Guess the covered word.

15 min.

Making Words is fun but continue to use your time after *Word Wall* some days for *Guess the Covered Word* lessons. **Some children never become really good at putting sounds together to decode a word but most words can be figured out if you look at the beginning letters, the length of the words and think about what words would make sense.** *Guess the Covered Word* **helps children develop this cross checking ability. For some children, this is their most successful decoding activity.** Here are just a few of the many possibilities. **Remember to use the names of your children and relate your sentences to what they are interested in.**

November

In November Mike watches **football**.

Heidi begins to wear a **sweater**.

Our class learns a lot about **Thanksgiving**.

Betty is baking a **pumpkin** pie.

Amy will **bring** the fruit.

Who will cook the **feast**?

The First Thanksgiving

The **Pilgrims** came to America on a ship.

It was a long hard **voyage** across the ocean.

Many people were **crowded** on the ship.

The Pilgrims **planted** their own food.

The natives helped them **plant**.

They all gave thanks for their **blessings**.

After reading *Those Can-Do Pigs**, you can write sentences summarizing the book:

Those Can-Do pigs can repair **chairs**.

Can-Do pigs like to make **music**.

Other Can-Do pigs fly like a **bird**.

A **broom** helps these pigs clean.

Snacks are what Can-Do pigs like to eat.

A Can-Do pig can be a good **friend**.

Math

We learn about **shapes** in math.

Sometimes **problems** are hard to do.

Often we make a **graph**.

Flashcards help us learn our facts.

We have to **practice** our addition facts.

Those Can-Do Pigs, by David McPhail. (Scholastic, 1996).

MAKING WORDS

⏱ 20 min.

Once you have done several easy *Making Words* lessons **you are ready to have lessons sorting for two-and three-letter beginning sounds, silent letters, and all the different spelling patterns and endings. Sorting for all these things helps children to see how words work and how to use letter sounds, spelling patterns, and endings when they are writing.** What follows are eight lessons for November. **These words were chosen because they fit into November themes.** You may want to sort for specific phonics elements that your students are learning. For additional *Making Words* lists and suggestions, refer to *Making Words*, by Cunningham & Hall (Good Apple, 1994) as well as *Making More Words*, by Cunningham & Hall (Good Apple, 1997). *Making More Words* is the easier of the two books and *Making Words* is a good choice to use in second grade once you have done several easy lessons and your children understand the procedure.

Secret word: November
Letters: e, e, o, b, m, n, r, v
Make: be, me, men, Ben, mob, rob, robe/bore, more, been, November
Sort: -en, -ob, -ore,
Transfer: when, snore, cob, throb

Secret word: turkeys
Letters: e, u, k, r, s, t, y
Make: us, use, set, yet, key, rut, ruts, rust, keys, true, rusty, turkeys
Sort: plurals, -et
Transfer: pet, vet, nets, jets

Secret word: Pilgrims
Letters: i, i, g, l, m, p, r, s
Make: is, lip, sip, rip, rig, pig, pigs, lips/slip, grip, girl, girls, Pilgrims
Sort: r-, p-, -ip, -ig, plurals
Transfer: ship, trip, dig, twig

Secret word: vegetables
Letters: a, e, e, e, b, g, l, s, t, v
Make: at, bat/tab, gab/bag, sag, sat, set,vet, leg, beg, beat, seat, table, vegetables
Sort: b-, s-, t-, -at, -ag, -ab, -et, -eg, -eat
Transfer: flag, grab, peg, yet

Secret word: potatoes
Letters: a, e, o, o, p, t, t, s
Make: as, at, to, tot, pot, pat, pet, set, sat, stop/post, paste, taste, teapot, potatoes
Sort: t-, p-, -at, -ot, -et, -aste
Transfer: hot, knot, wet, waste

Secret word: Mayflower
Letters: a, e, o, f, l, m, r, w, y
Make: am, ram, yam/may, ray, way, lay, row, mow, low, flow, fray, flower, Mayflower
Sort: m-, fl-, -am, -ay, -ow
Transfer: slam, tray, clay, slow

Secret word: Thanksgiving
Letters: a, i, i, g, g, h, k, n, s, t, v
Make: an, at, it, in, tin, tan/ant, van, vain, gain, sank, tank, thank, Thanksgiving
Sort: -in, -an, -ain, -ank
Transfer: plan, stain, plain, Frank

Secret word: dinner
Letters: e, i, d, n, n, r
Make: in, inn, end/Ned/den, die, red, rid, ride, rind, dine, nine, diner, dinner
Sort: d-, r-, -in-inn (homophones), -ed, -ine
Transfer: Ted, shed, pine, spine

READING/WRITING RHYMES

20 min.

Reading/Writing Rhymes is another activity which helps students learn to use patterns to decode and spell hundreds of words. In addition, all beginning sounds (onsets) are reviewed every time you do a *Reading/Writing Rhymes* lesson. Once all the rhyming words are generated on a chart, the teacher, along with her students, write some rhymes using these words and then read each other's rhymes. Because writing and reading are connected to every lesson, students learn how you use these patterns as you actually read and write.

For *Reading/Writing Rhymes*, you will need an onset deck (3"x 5" index cards) containing 50 beginning letter cards including:

- Single consonants: b, c, d, f, g, h, j, k, l, m, n, p, r, s, t, v, w, y, z

- Digraphs (two letters, one sound): sh, ch, th, wh

- Other two-letter, one sound combinations: ph, wr, kn, qu

- Blends (beginning letters blended together, sometimes called clusters): bl, br, cl, cr, dr, fl, fr, gl, gr, pl, pr, sc, scr, sk, sl, sm, sn, sp, spr, st, str, sw, tr

Here's how we do a *Reading/Writing Rhymes* lesson.

- **At the beginning of the lesson, we distribute all the onset cards to the students.** Depending on the number of students in your class, you distribute **one, two, or three cards to each student.**

- Once all the onset cards are distributed, we write the spelling pattern we are working with 10-12 times on a piece of chart paper. As we write it each time, we have the children help spell it and write it.

"__ack" chart		
__ack	__ack	__ack
__ack	__ack	__ack
__ack	__ack	__ack
__ack	__ack	__ack

- We then invite children, who have a card that they think will make a word, to come up and place their card next to one of the written spelling patterns and pronounce the word.

- If the word is indeed a real word, we use the word in a sentence and write that word on the chart by adding the beginning letter(s) on the line in front of an <u>ack</u> spelling pattern.

- If the word is not a real word, we explain why we cannot write it on a chart.

- If the word is a real word and does rhyme but has a different spelling pattern, such as yak to rhyme with <u>ack</u>, we explain that it rhymes but has a different spelling pattern, and we include it at the bottom of the chart with an asterisk next to it.

- We write names with capital letters, and if a word can be a name and not a name, such as J<u>ack</u> and j<u>ack</u>, we write it both ways.

- When all the children who think they can spell words with their beginning letters and the spelling pattern have come up, we call children up to make the words not yet there by saying something like:

  "I think the person with the **sl** card could come up here and add **sl** to <u>ack</u> to make a word we know."

- We try to include all the words that any of our children would have in their listening vocabulary but avoid any obscure words.

- If the patterns for words that we wrote to begin our chart get made into complete words, we add as many more patterns as needed to write all the words we can make.

- Finally, if we can think of some good longer words that rhyme and have that spelling pattern, we add them to the list.

- We spell and write the whole word on the chart under the other words we have on our chart because the children do not have the extra spelling patterns needed to spell it with their onset cards.

"__ack" chart		
b<u>ack</u>	J<u>ack</u>	cr<u>ack</u>
sn<u>ack</u>	j<u>ack</u>	r<u>ack</u>
t<u>ack</u>	bl<u>ack</u>	st<u>ack</u>
tr<u>ack</u>	p<u>ack</u>	l<u>ack</u>
qu<u>ack</u>	s<u>ack</u>	sh<u>ack</u>
wh<u>ack</u>	sl<u>ack</u>	fl<u>ack</u>
h<u>ack</u>	kn<u>ack</u>	sm<u>ack</u>
		*yak
		*plaque

Once the chart of rhyming words is written, **we work together in a shared writing format to write a couple of sentences using lots of the rhyming words.** After generating all the rhyming words, a class came up with this silly rhyme:

Jack went back to the shack near the track

to have a snack from his black backpack.

Next the students write rhymes. Many teachers let them work in pairs or teams to write these rhymes and then read their rhymes to the class.

Alisha's and Ashley's Writing Sample

> Mack, Jack, and Zack had a fun time running around the track. Mack and Jack told the duck to quack. Mack had a sack on his back. Zack stayed back. Zack ate a snack in an old black shack.

Amy's Writing Sample

> Jack and Zack went out back to eat their snack but Zack stepped on a crack and broke his back. Jack took Zack to Dr. Mack and he said he broke his back. Zack sat in a chair but he sat on a thumb tack, it hurt so bad he ran out the front door and ran the track. He ran so fast he started to quack. He quacked so hard he bumbed into Jack. Jack had to go to Dr. Mack 'cause Zack headed for the tool shack.

You can do *Reading/Writing Rhymes* lessons to teach any common spelling pattern. Here are some of the words students might use with the patterns **at**, **ad**, **et**, **en**.

"-at" words

at, bat, cat, hat, fat, flat, gnat, mat, pat, rat, sat, splat, that

---

"-ad" words

bad, Chad, clad, dad, fad, grad, had, lad, mad, pad, sad, tad, *add, *plaid

---

"-et" words

bet, get, jet, let, met, net, pet, set, vet, wet, yet, *debt, *sweat, *threat

---

"-en" words

Ben, den, hen, men, pen, ten, then, when, Glen, Gwen, *been

How *Reading/Writing Rhymes* is Multilevel

Reading/Writing Rhymes is a multilevel activity in much the same way that *Making Words* is multilevel. **The oral concept of rhyme and the idea that words that rhyme usually have the same spelling are reviewed in each lesson. All beginning letters (onsets) are reviewed, and, if students need lots of practice with these, you can have them say the sound for each onset as you hand them out.** If you have some children still struggling with the simplest beginning sounds, give them the single consonant cards and give the more complex onset cards to your more sophisticated readers. **Adding some common words with different spelling patterns helps your students develop a "set for diversity" and reminds them that when dealing with English patterns, we have to think "usually," not "always." Also, as your students write rhymes using the chart of words, they write on a variety of levels, but they all enjoy it.** Be sure you remind your students about spelling the *Word Wall* words correctly when writing "everything." When we watch children who have teachers that enforced this rule, the children do this automatically. They know that **said** is not spelled like **Ted.** It is a *Word Wall* word and spelled **s-a-i-d**.

APPLYING STRATEGIES WHEN READING AND WRITING

Remember to make sure that your students are reading books on "their own level" during Self-Selected Reading time. All students in second grade should be "really" reading (reading all the words) if the right books are available. If some of your students cannot find a good book, (whether a chapter book or one written for an emergent reader) it may mean that these children will have to go to the library in your school or bring a book from home. The students who still need easy, predictable books also need a chance to read and reread these books at school. Speed and accuracy come with practice and so does fluency. Children know when they are making progress and some daily independent reading helps them develop these skills. This is also a good time for some students to reread stories or books you read as a class or with a small group at the beginning of the year. You will be surprised and so will your students when they see that what was once "hard" to read is much easier now—they must be getting smarter. So give the children a chance by putting those books and stories in your book baskets or on your library shelf for them to enjoy "one more time."

The end of the month is once again time to take stock of those children who started the month behind their peers in what they know about words. In most second-grade classrooms, teachers have focused some attention on these areas with particular children during daily reading, writing, *Word Wall*, and other word activities. Even children who were struggling are making visible progress. Remember that it is progress you are assessing. Some children are going to take longer than others to develop these abilities, but if we see month-to-month growth based on our nudges during daily activities, we know that they will eventually develop these critical understandings. For children who are making progress, but are still not there yet, continue the kind of individual nudging you have been doing for as long as necessary. **Our experience with "won't give up" teachers tells us that second graders can eventually catch up if we do not give up! The question is not "IF?" but "WHEN?" The answer depends on your will power and determination to continue to assess and nudge.**

DECEMBER

December at school is always a busy month. Parents are busy, children are busy, and teachers are busy! Everyone is excited and everyone has a lot to do. There are holidays to get ready for and a vacation from school will cut this month shorter than most. It is hard to keep to any kind of a schedule but children learn best when they have a routine.

Working with Words, along with the other three blocks, should continue. However, most teachers would not introduce a new activity this month. They would indeed use the excitement of what is going on to keep the children interested in learning. Here are some activities for December you can get done along with all the seasonal fun!

MONTH AT A GLANCE

By the end of December, you will have reviewed the following:

- Reviewing *Word Wall* words by writing new words that rhyme

- Using holiday words on a theme board to write sentences

- *Guess the Covered Word* lessons with holiday (theme board) words

- *Making Words* lessons with less cueing by the teacher

- Coaching during writing

WORD WALL

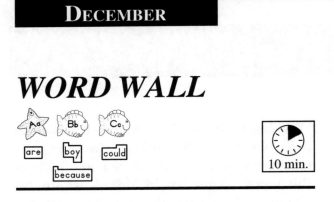

10 min.

ON THE BACK ACTIVITY (EXTENDING 5 *WORD WALL* WORDS TO OTHER RHYMING WORDS)

5 min.

December is a good time to review all those words that are on the *Word Wall* along with adding a few new ones. Imagine that you have 5 words to review: **car, make, skate, truck, clock**. After writing the *Word Wall* words and self-correcting them, your students are ready to turn their papers over to the back.

The teacher then asks the students to write.

1. On the top of my tree is a **star**. (Students are asked which *Word Wall* word will help.) They decide that the word **car** will help and use the "**ar**" pattern to help them write **star**.

2. Mom will **bake** cookies for Christmas. (Students are asked which *Word Wall* word will help them write **bake**.) They decide that the word **make** will help and use the "**ake**" pattern to help them write **bake**.

3. We leave Santa a **plate** of cookies. (Students are asked which *Word Wall* word will help.) They decide that the word **skate** will help and use the "**ate**" pattern to help them write **plate**.

4. I hope Santa will not get **stuck** in the chimney. (Students are asked which *Word Wall* word will help.) They decide that the word **truck** will help and use the "**uck**" pattern to help them write **stuck**.

5. My **stocking** is red and very big. (Students are asked which *Word Wall* word will help.) They decide that the word **clock** will help and use the "**ock**" pattern and the ending "**ing**" to help them write **stocking**.

On-the-Back Activity (Using Theme Words)

In addition to the *Word Wall*, **most teachers have a theme board that relates to the particular theme being studied.** In addition to pictures on the board, the theme board contains words that help children when they choose to write about the things they are learning while studying that theme. Imagine that you have a Happy Holidays theme board in your room, and it contains pictures and words such as:

Holidays:
Christmas
Hanukkah
Kwanzaa
New Year's

December:
winter
snow
vacation
gifts
presents
Santa
reindeer
sleigh
decorations
candles
celebrate

and/or others appropriate for your children.

You can work on their sentence writing skills as well as have them practicing *Word Wall* words and theme words. On some days dictate a sentence or two that is made up of words from your *Word Wall* and the theme board. Depending on what words you have on the wall and the board, you might include sentences such as:

This is **December**.

Christmas is coming.

Some people **celebrate Kwanzaa** at this time.

Others **celebrate Hanukkah**.

People get ready for the **holidays**.

Many homes have **decorations**.

The teacher says the sentence while the children listen and decide which word is on the theme board. The children then see the word on the theme board (**visual**). Next, they cheer or chant the spelling of the word (**auditory**). Finally, they write the word (**kinesthetic**). The teacher writes the word along with the children. They self-correct the word and trace around its shape following the teacher's lead. Children love to write about the holidays. Learning how to use words from the theme board and the *Word Wall* to write sentences helps move them along in their independent writing ability. It also helps the students remember that the spelling of holiday words is easy if they just "read the room."

ROUNDING UP THE RHYMES

⏱ 20 min.

A rhyming book children love is Carol Diggory Shields's *Saturday Night at the Dinosaur Stomp* (Scholastic, 1997). This book **describes dinosaurs getting ready for the Saturday night dance.** These dinosaurs are just like people in how they think and feel and even enjoy the volcano's fireworks. **The first reading is to enjoy the book. The second reading may be an echo reading—you reading a line and the children echoing the line after you have read it.** Keep a good beat and they will not only follow, they will enjoy it. After that, you may want to ask, "Did this really happen?" The third reading of the book may be an appropriate time to call the children's attention to the wonderful rhyming words. **As you read each page again, encourage the children to listen for the rhymes as you say them. As children identify the rhyming words, write them on index cards and put them in a pocket chart or on an overhead transparency.**

"Word went out 'cross the prehistoric **slime**:

Hey, dinosaurs, it's rock 'n' roll **time**!

Slick back your scales and get ready to **romp**

On Saturday night at the Dinosaur **Stomp**!"

The children should be able to tell you that **slime** and **time,** along with **romp** and **stomp,** are the rhyming words on the first two pages. Write those four words on index cards and put them in the pocket chart. Some teachers use the chalkboard, others use an overhead transparency. **The important thing is that once they *hear* the rhymes they can then *see* the rhyming words. Some of the rhyming words will have the same spelling pattern (*slime* and *time*) and some will not (*shore* and *floor*).** When you are finished writing the rhyming pairs, it will look like this:

slime	romp	shore
time	stomp	floor
nails	splash	eggs
tails	bash	legs
Maiasaur	bunch	stared
four	punch	scared
three	Ultrasauras	back
tree	chorus	whack
rhyme	chance	bump
time	dance	jump
line	glow	shake
behind	show	earthquake
outrageous	beat	swamp
Cretaceous	feet	stomp

Notice how some of the rhyming pairs have the same spelling pattern and others do not. **Have the children help you cross out or discard rhyming pairs that do not have the same spelling pattern.** When you finish you will have these pairs left:

slime	romp	nails
time	stomp	tails
splash	bunch	stared
bash	punch	scared
three	back	chance
tree	whack	dance
bump	glow	shake
jump	show	earthquake
outrageous		
Creataceous		

Finally, we do a transfer step and remind the children that thinking of rhyming words can help them when they are reading and writing. This transfer step is an important part of the lesson if you want them to use what they know about words when they come to an unknown word in their reading and writing.

"What if you were reading and came to this word?" (Show **dime**, don't say it.) "What words in the pocket chart would help you read that word? Yes, **slime** and **time** have the same spelling pattern and rhyme. Let's see . . . **d—ime**." (Model this thinking and separating of sounds so that children will understand what you do when you come to a word and you know the spelling pattern but not the word.) "The word is **dime**. The candy cane cost a **dime**."

What if you were writing and wanted to write that you saw a **snowflake** you caught on your mitten. What spelling pattern would help. Yes, the "**ake**" spelling pattern in **shake** and **earthquake**. You may want to do this again with **hunch** and **glance**.

The books we read to our class can be used to further the children's word knowledge. Look for holiday books written in rhyme. There are many of these books in libraries and at the bookstores at this time of year.

GUESS THE COVERED WORD

Guess the covered **word.**

15 min.

Continue to present *Guess the Covered Word* lessons. Let the holidays and all the celebrations keep your students involved. Using their names makes the sentences even better! You can also use the books and stories you have been reading to the class. Remember to have a variety of on-sets (beginning letters).

December

My favorite holiday is **Hanukkah**.

The menorah is **bright** when lighted.

Christmas is another holiday in December.

Children get **presents** in December.

The holidays are **special** for families.

Holiday Gifts

Jeanne wants a new **sled**.

Kathy always needs new **skates**.

Chrisy wants some **skis**.

Mom's **gloves** need to be replaced.

Franny wishes for **jewelry**.

Dad wants a new **shovel**.

Keeping Warm

Karen wears a **sweater**.

Matthew wears his **jacket**.

A **sweatshirt** will keep you warm.

Kristen's **mittens** keep her warm.

Billy's **shirt** is made of wool.

Everyone likes a **scarf** when it gets cold.

Holiday Cookies

Grandma's cookies are the best.

She always lets **Stephanie** help her.

Joey's favorite is her **chocolate** cookies.

Sometimes Pat makes **cinnamon** cookies.

Mom likes **cocoa** with her cookies.

But, David likes **milk**.

MAKING WORDS

⏱ 20 min.

If you started *Making Words* in October and did a number of easy lessons with five letters and just one or two vowels, the children were probably ready to move into lessons that have 6-8 letters, including two vowels in November. **As we continue to make words, we do less cueing than we did in early lessons. For example, in early lessons, we say, "Change the last letter…" But, as we move along, we want the children to think about what letters to change, and we would be more apt to say, "Change just one letter…"** Here is an example of a good December lesson **with seven letters, two vowels and less cueing:**

Secret word: candles

Letters: a, e, c, d, l, n, s

Make:

- "Take two letters and make **as**. Do it **as** quickly **as** possible."

- "Change a letter to make the word **an**. I will get **an** ornament at the store."

- "Now add one letter and make the three-letter word **can**. You **can** do that."

- "Now make the three-letter word **and**. I will buy a gift for Dad **and** Mom."

- "Add a letter to make the four-letter word **sand**. You need **sand** when it is slippery outside."

- " Change a letter and you have **land**. The **land** was covered with snow."

- "Make one more four-letter word **clan**. Our **clan** (another word for family) will come for the holidays."

- "Add one letter and you can make the five-letter word **clean**. We will **clean** the house for the holidays."

- "Start with new letters and make the word **dance**. I watched the people **dance** in the Nutcracker."

- "Now just one more letter and **dance** becomes **dances**. Make the word **dances**."

- "Let's make another six-letter word **cleans**. Sue **cleans** the house before company comes."

- "Now use all the letters to make the secret word."

- "Has anyone figured out the secret word?" (Look around the room and see if someone has the word in their letter cardholder.) "The secret word is **candles**. People light **candles** to celebrate the holiday season." Have someone who has made the word **candles** come to the pocket chart and make it with the large letter cards. Then have the other students check/correct this final word.

Sort:

- Now you are ready for the second step—sorting. When the children have made **candles**, we draw their attention to the words they made; these are the words that are still in the pocket chart on index cards. You then help them sort for a variety of patterns. Take the word **clan** and have them find the other words that begin with **cl—clean, cleans.**

- Next help them to sort the words into rhymes:

an	and
can	sand
clan	land

- You can also sort for "related" words. "Can you find two related words?"

- Lead the children to find that **clean** and **cleans** are related.

- Can you find two more?"

- Lead the class to see that **dance** and **dances** are related.

Transfer:

- The third step is the transfer step. Remind the children that rhyming words can help them read and spell words. Write two words and have them use the sorted rhymes to decode them:

plan	sandman

- Say a few rhyming words and have them decide how they would spell them:

clan	handstand

Here are a few other seasonal lessons:

Secret word: Rudolph
Letters: o, u, d, h, l, p, r
Make: do, up, ho, hop, our, old, hold, hour, drop, uphold/holdup, Rudolph
Sort: h-, -op, -old, -our
Transfer: shop, cold, scold, sour

Secret word: holidays
Letters: a, i, o, d, h, l, s, y
Make: as, is, his, has, had, hay, lay, old, hold, sold, lash, dash, daily, daisy, holidays
Sort: h-, d-, -ay, -ash, -old
Transfer: pray, cash, trash, gold

Secret word: ornament
Letters: a, e, o, m, n, n, r, t
Make: or, on, am, ram, arm, are, eat, neat, meat, mean, meant, ornament
Sort: m-, -am, -eat
Transfer: jam, scram, seat, neat

Secret word: Christmas
Letters: a, i, c, h, m, r, s, s, t
Make: it, hit, sit, sat, hat, rat/art, mart, chat, cart, chart, start, Chris, charts, Christmas
Sort: c-, ch-, chr-, -it, -at, -art, plurals
Transfer: smart, dart, knit, skit

Secret word: packages
Letters: a, a, e, c, g, k, p, s
Make: as, sag, gas, peg, keg, age, ages/sage, sack, pack, page, cage, cages, pages, packages
Sort: s-, c-, p-, -eg, -age, -ack
Transfer: beg, stage, crack, track

READING/WRITING RHYMES

20 min.

We will **work on short vowel patterns this month** with some *Reading and Writing Rhymes*. One pattern that is "fun" during December is the "**op**" pattern. Write "_op" ten times and have the children come up to the chart and place a beginning letter(s) in front of the rhyme to show the beginning sounds that added to the spelling pattern makes a word they know. The teacher adds these to the chart:

"__op" chart		
bop	hop	shop
chop	mop	stop
cop	mop	stop
crop	plop	top
drop	pop	
flop	prop	
		*swap

Next, they write a silly rhyme, such as:

> Let's **stop** and **shop** for **Pop**.
>
> Don't buy a **mop**, that will be a **flop**!

Finally, let the children write rhymes by themselves or in pairs, then let some children share their rhymes and the other children have fun listening.

Here are some short vowel patterns to work on this month and the rhyming words they generate. Those with a * rhyme but do not have the same spelling pattern.

"-ill" words
bill, dill, chill, drill, fill, grill, hill, ill, Jill, kill, mill, Phil, pill, sill, skill, still, thrill, will, anthill, fulfill, uphill

"-ot" words
blot, cot, clot, dot, got, knot, lot, not, plot, pot, rot, shot, slot, spot, tot, trot

"-ug" words
bug, chug, drug, hug, jug, lug, mug, plug, pug, rug, shrug, slug, smug, snug, thug, tug, *ugh

"-ut" words
but, cut, gut, hut, nut, rut, shut, smut, strut, *putt, *what, *mutt

Here is a rhyme for the "**-ill**" pattern:

> Bill had his fill of dill and got ill. He took a pill for the chill. Then, he sat on the window sill and watched his Dad grill with skill.

APPLYING STRATEGIES WHEN READING AND WRITING

Coaching During Writing

The first opportunity to help children each day one-on-one is during the *Writing Block*. **In second grade, children write every day but not every piece is taken to final copy. It should not be! Every piece a writer writes is not always edited and published. There are many words that children write that they can't be expected to spell, and when you conference with them simply acknowledge their attempt and write it correctly.** For other words, such as those on the *Word Wall* or those words with familiar spelling patterns, they should be using what they know to get the correct spelling. It is these words that we mention during our conference too. "This word is on the *Word Wall*—you should have written it correctly. Do it now. These words have spelling patterns we have learned when doing *On-the-Back* activities. If you use the word **ride**, you can figure out the word **slide**." Writing conferences are a good time to help children use what they have learned to write lots of other words. The writing conference is not always an editing conference. If students still need help getting thoughts on paper, that is what you help them with. If students are writing run-on sentences that is what they get help with.

During a writing conference everyone gets what he or she needs. It isn't always an editing conference—but sometimes it could be!

Coaching During Reading

The second way to assist children to use what they know while they are reading is to conduct individual or small group conferences when they are reading. When a child comes to a word and stops, say:

- "Put your finger on the word and say all the letters." Good readers look at all the letters in a word automatically; that is why they get the words right. Missing one letter would change most words!

- Then remind them to, "Keep a finger on the word and finish the sentence." This way the child can easily track back and find the word.

- If the child still does not know the word, remind him to use any picture clues that might be on the page.

- If the troublesome word can be decoded with one of the spelling patterns on the *Word Wall* you could say, "Let's see if you can use house to help you read blouse?"

Helping children see that they can use what they know to figure out words they don't know is important for some children. For other children, you will notice that they use known words to figure out unknown words with little or no coaching.

The year has come to an end—but not the school year. Most teachers are anxious to return after the holidays because they see those late bloomers beginning to bloom!

Happy New Year! **January begins a new year as well as some old activities with a new twist.** People in many parts of the country are experiencing short days and long nights. The weather is cold and many days we simply have to stay inside. Reading and writing are good activities to fill those long winter nights. Share with your students the book you are reading now (if you can) and the books you loved when you were young. Let them learn more about winter— especially if they do not see snow in your part of the country—by reading informational books on what animals and people do in the winter. Children can also learn from good fiction books like *The Snowy Day* by Ezra Jack Keats (Puffin Books, 1996). Penguins, hibernation, snowstorms, skiing, and shoveling snow are all "winter" subjects which help students learn about their world. Winter is a cold but magical time—even without the snow.

The first weeks of January are a great time for learning in school. Many teachers come back from the holidays and notice that their students who were struggling are now reading grade-level material. When did it happen? It is almost as if they were given this gift for their holiday present—it just did not come in a package. It is a wonderful time to continue on this literacy journey. Your work is paying off! **They are rested and ready to learn even more.**

MONTH AT A GLANCE

By the end of January, you will have reviewed the following:

- *Guess the Covered Word* lesson with an emphasis on 2 and 3 letter blends

- *Making Words* lessons with an emphasis on 2 and 3 letter blends and changing letters around to make a new and different word

- How to plan your own *Making Words* lesson

- *Reading/Writing Rhymes* with an emphasis on long vowel patterns

- Assessing word strategies used in reading, writing, and spelling at the midpoint of second grade

WORD WALL

10 min.

The *Word Wall* is growing. Most second-grade *Word Wall*s should have 60-70 high-frequency words by the end of January. If you were to watch a teacher do the daily *Word Wall* activity of calling out five words for the children to locate, clap or cheer for, and write, you might conclude that all the children were learning the same thing—how to spell the words. But your conclusion would be wrong! *Word Wall* is actually a multilevel activity because different children are at all different stages of their word learning. **For those who have already learned to read the words added to the wall, they are learning to spell them!** But unless your classroom is quite different from most second grades, not all your children learned to read all of the *Word Wall* words during their reading last year and this year. **Some children need a whole lot of practice to learn to read these important high-frequency words. When we call out words for the children to locate, clap or cheer for, and write, some children are getting the added practice they require to be able, eventually, to read these words anywhere they see them.** Once they have learned to read these words—which might take several weeks or even months of practice— the very same *Word Wall* activity through which they learned to read them becomes the vehicle for them to learn to **spell** them. Meanwhile, the children know which words are on the wall and can locate words they need to spell when writing. In most classrooms, the rule is: "Spell words the best you can but if the word is on the *Word Wall*, you have to spell it right!"

There are also a few children in every second grade that are such fast word learners that they learned to both read and spell the words during last week's reading of a selection in which these words occurred! What are they learning from the daily *Word Wall* activity? These **super word learners are one of the reasons most teachers combine handwriting instruction with the writing of the *Word Wall* words.** Even fast word learners in second grade need reminders and modeling of how to make the letters so that their writing can be easily read.

ON-THE-BACK ACTIVITY (REVIEWING RHYMING WORDS)

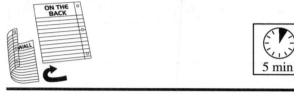

5 min.

The *On-the-Back* activity also helps even the fastest word learners. **We have talked about showing children how some of the *Word Wall* words can help them read and spell lots of rhyming words.** We would continue all year to have the children turn their *Word Wall* papers over and do something like this:

"All the *Word Wall* words help you spell when you are writing. In fact, the reason that we are putting up these words is that you see them over and over again when you are reading and use them over and over again when you are writing. It would be impossible to read and write without knowing our *Word Wall* words. **Some of the *Word Wall* words (starred or stickered in most classrooms) are particularly helpful words because they help you spell lots of rhyming words.** Let's work on that today. **One of the *Word Wall* words you practiced to-day was name. I am going to tell you some sentences to write that have words that rhyme with name. You listen for the rhyming word and then we will decide together how to spell that word.** What if you were writing:

Soccer is my favorite **game.**

Yes, the word that rhymes with **name** is **game,** and we know that words that rhyme usually have the same spelling pattern. Let's write the first letter we hear in **game**, **g**, and then the spelling pattern in **name**, so we add **a-m-e** to spell the rhyming word **game**."

The lesson continues with the teacher saying a sentence that uses one word that rhymes with **name** and is spelled **a-m-e**.

My mother put my new picture in a **frame**.
We cooked our hot dogs over the **flame**.
When our team lost, I felt I was to **blame**.
Some kids have the **same** friends.

Notice that with these words, there could be another spelling pattern (*aim*) that rhymes. That is precisely the reason that we come up with the examples rather than ask the children to give us rhyming words. We are trying to teach them that most words that rhyme have the same spelling pattern. If we ask them for rhymes, they are apt to volunteer *aim* and *claim,* and then they won't understand why they don't work. If they do ask about other words, you can tell them that some rhymes have other possible spellings. When this happens you just have to know which one looks right to tell which one to use, but, at this point, we are happy if they begin to realize that spell-ing is not letter-by-letter, but rather is related to patterns. A second grader who notices two or more spelling patterns for a rhyme is ahead of a child who is still "sound spelling" all the words that are not on the *Word Wall*.

So, to avoid the confusion, we offer the examples, they decide which word rhymes, and we all decide how to spell it. This activity moves the good word learners along in their ability to decode and spell words not yet learned. It is also good phonemic awareness training for children still struggling with the oral concept of rhyme.

Some *Word Wall* rhymes to work with this month could be:

> For **about** you can write **pout, scout, shout, sprout,** and **trout.**
>
> For **bug** you can write **dug, mug, hug, jug,** and **shrug**.
>
> For **crash** you can write **dash, flash, rash, trash,** and **splash**.
>
> For **drink** you can write **blink, mink, stink, shrink**, and **think**.
>
> For **float** you can write **boat, coat, gloat, goat,** and **throat**.
>
> For **found** you could write **ground, hound, pound, sound,** and **around**.
>
> For **house** you can write **blouse, mouse, spouse, doghouse,** and **outhouse**.
>
> For **joke** you can write **broke, choke, spoke, stroke,** and **woke**.

GUESS THE COVERED WORD — WITH BLENDS

Guess the covered word.

15 min.

Guess the Covered Word lessons in which some of the targeted words begin with a single letter and some begin with two or more letters are important in second grade. You can hear the beginning letters if you say the word slowly. Be sure that when you uncover the beginning letters, you uncover everything up to the vowel. If you have uncovered an **s** and a child guesses the word **snow**, tell the child that was good thinking for the **s**. Then, have everyone say **snow** slowly and hear the **s** and **n**. "**My rule is that I have to show you everything up to the vowel,** so if the word were **snow**, I would have to show you not just the **s** but the **n,** too."

Here are some *Guess the Covered Word* lessons appropriate for January. The best lessons are those that you make yourself to follow up on whatever your class is learning. Many teachers keep these on a chart tablet, covering the target words with self-adhesive notes so they can be reused the next year.

Winter Weather

In winter it is often **snowy**.

David watches the weather on TV.

Sarah wants to know if it will **change**.

When it **freezes** it is sometimes hard to drive.

People always get **groceries** before a storm.

Snowman

Kim will make the **snowballs**.

Rusty has a **scarf** for him.

Mary has the **cherry** for his nose.

Bob has **branches** for his arms.

Betty's **sweater** makes him look real.

Animals in Winter

The bears are **hibernating** in caves.

The birds have flown south in a **flock**.

Many animals are under the **ground**.

Others have eaten and are **sleeping**.

In winter many animals **scavenge** for food.

Martin Luther King, Jr.

Martin Luther King Jr. was a great **speaker**.

He **fought** for civil rights.

He worked hard for **freedom** for all.

Brandon has a **video** about Dr. King.

There are many **stories** about him.

Brittany says, "He was a great **leader**."

Sea Otters*

Sea otters **dive** for their food.

They hold **food** with their front paws.

They take food to the **surface** to eat.

They lie on their **backs** when they eat.

Sea Otters, by Avelyn Davidson. (Shortland Publications, 1998).

MAKING WORDS— AN EMPHASIS ON BLENDS

20 min.

In December, **we talked about choosing the "secret word" to tie in with a theme, unit, or seasonal activity. Another criteria for choosing a "secret word" is that it allows you to have specific examples from which to sort.** Here are some lessons in which **all the words begin with a two-letter blend or with one of those two letters. There are also many words they will have to stretch out to hear the two sounds as they spell the words at their desks.**

1. First, sort them according to their beginning letters—everything up to the vowel.

2. Then, say some other words that begin with the blend or with one of the other letters and have children decide how they would begin to spell the word.

3. Finally, sort out the rhymes and give them a few words to read and spell that rhyme and have the same spelling pattern. This will help them transfer their word skills when they are actually reading and writing.

4. For the transfer words, we continue to use two and three letter blends.

Secret word: snowman
Letters: a, o, m, n, n, s, w
Make: am, an, man, Sam, saw/was*, won/now/own*, sown/snow*, swan, swam, woman, snowman
Sort: sn-, sw-, -am, -an, -own
Transfer: scram, plan, grown, flown
  * This lesson offers children a chance to see that, when letters are moved around, you can make new words.

Secret word: snowball
Letters: a, o, b, l, n, s, w
Make: so, no, was/saw, own, bow, low, blow, slow, slaw, ball, balls, bowls/blows, blow, snowball
Sort: sl-, bl-, -o, -ow, -aw, -own
Transfer: go, grow, straw, flown

Secret word: mountains
Letters: a, i, o, u, m, n, n, t, s
Make: in, at, sat, mat, man, tan, tin, ton/not, into, tuna, Stan, stain, mount, amount, mountains
Sort: st-, -at, -in, -an, -ount
Transfer: flat, spin, than, count

Secret word: blizzards
Letters: a, i, b, d, l, r, s, z, z
Make: is, lid, lad, lab, lid, bid, bad, sad, slab, drab/Brad, raid, braid, lizard, blizzards
Sort: br, -ad, -ab, -aid
Transfer: glad, Chad, grab, maid

Secret word: penquins
Letters: e, i, u, g, n, n, p, s
Make: us, is, in, pin, pig, peg, pen, pens, spin, pine, spine, penguins
Sort: p-, sp-, -in, -ine
Transfer: twin, skin, vine, twine

Secret word: football
Letters: a, o, o, b, f, l, l, t
Make: at, bat, fat, fall, ball, tall, boot, loot/tool, fool, flat, boat, float, football
Sort: fl-, -at, -oot, -ool, -oat
Transfer: splat, shoot, scoot, throat

Secret word: cheering
Letters: e, e, i, c, g, h, n, r
Make: in, he, hen, her, ice, nice, rice, rich, inch, grin, chin, cheer, nicer, enrich, cheering
Sort: ch-, gr-, -in, -ice
Transfer: twin, twice, slice, price

Planning Your Own *Making Words* Lessons

It is fun to plan your own *Making Words* lessons to fit in with themes. Here are the steps to go through to plan a lesson:

1. Decide what the "secret word" is that can be made with all the letters. In choosing this word, consider books the children are reading, theme words, and words that tie into something you are doing at school. Also, think about the letter sounds and patterns you want to call attention to during the sorting and transferring steps at the end.

2. Make a list of the words students can make from these letters.

3. From all the words you could make, pick approximately 15 words that include the following:

    a. words that can be sorted for spelling patterns you want to emphasize

    b. little words and big words so that the lesson is a multilevel lesson

    c. words that can be made by arranging the same letters in a different way (stop/post) to remind the children that when spelling words, the ordering of the letters is crucial

    d. a name or two to remind them that names need capital letters

    e. words that most students have in their listening vocabularies

4. Write all the words on index cards in the order from shortest to longest.

5. Sequence the index cards to emphasize letter patterns or to reflect how changing the position of the letters or changing/adding just one letter results in a different word. Write each transfer word on an index card.

6. Store the cards in an envelope. On the envelope, first write the words in the order you will make them, next the patterns you will sort for, and finally several words for the transfer activity.

READING/WRITING RHYMES

20 min.

We have found that *Reading/Writing Rhymes* is popular with second-grade students. **Teachers tell us the children love making up silly rhymes using as many words as they can from the list generated using the onset deck (the 50 beginning sounds) and the "rime" or spelling pattern. The spelling pattern is chosen because the teacher wants to cover all the short and long vowel patterns.** Last month, we chose our patterns to work on some familiar short vowel spelling patterns. **This month we will work on *ay, ake, ail, ale, aid,* and *ade*.** Teachers also report that children are thinking as they choose words: "Does that have the right spelling pattern? Is that a *Word Wall* word?" What we see is an amazingly correct spelling for the young students who have learned to think about words and spelling patterns in a sophisticated way.

This is a list of words you can use for the **ay** pattern. Remember the * means it "rhymes" but does not have the same "rime" spelling pattern.

1. First, you make an **ay** chart, writing **ay** at least 10 times.

2. Next, you pass out the onset deck. (Most teachers make them on index cards and use them again and again.)

3. The children then bring the cards up and hold the beginning letters that make words, in front of the chart, and say the word.

4. When they have letters ("dr") that don't make words with the **ay** spelling pattern, they just give that card to the teacher.

5. Sometimes the teacher has to tell them that it will make a word—and give them a definition.

6. Other times she has to explain that the beginning letters are right but the word is spelled with a different spelling pattern. She then writes that word beside or below an asterisk.

"__ay" chart		
bay	pay	tray
bray	play	way
clay	pray	Jay
day	ray	Gay
fray	say	Ray
gay	slay	*hey
gray	spray	*neigh
hay	stay	*prey
lay	stray	*sleigh
may	sway	*they
		*weigh

7. Now, it is time for the fun—writing a silly rhyme with the children. Here is one they came up with:

> <u>Kay</u> and <u>Jay</u> went out to <u>play</u>.
> They went to the <u>bay</u>.
> They did not <u>stay</u> because the <u>day</u>
> was <u>gray</u>.

8. Finally, the children write the rhymes by themselves or with a partner. Listen to the conversation between partners and you realize how much the students profit from this cooperative work. Have three or four children read their rhymes and you will see how much your students think as they write.

Here are some other patterns, including the words you can make, when doing *Reading/Writing Rhymes* this month. Many rhyming words can be spelled with **ail** or **ale**. The same thing is true for **aid** and **ade**. The fact that there are two common patterns is not a problem when reading. Students quickly learn that both **ail** and **ale** often have the long **a** sound. When spelling a word, however, there is no way to know which one is the correct spelling unless you recognize it as a word you know after writing it. This is why we often write a word and then think, "That doesn't look right," and then try writing it with the other pattern to see if that looks right. When we write rhymes which have two common spelling patterns, we write both patterns on the same chart. Students come up and tell us the word their beginning letters will make and we write it with the correct pattern. In many cases, there are two homophones, words that are spelled differently and have different meanings but the same pronunciation. We write both of these and talk about what each one means. Artistic teachers draw a little picture next to one of these so that students can tell them apart.

"-ake" words:
bake, Blake, cake, fake, flake, Jake, lake, make, quake, rake, sake, shake, snake stake, take, wake, *ache, *break, *steak

"-ail" / "-ale" words:
bail, fail, frail, hail, jail, mail, nail, pail, quail, rail, sail, tail, trail, wail, *Braille, *veil

ale, bale, gale, male, pale, sale, scale, stale, tale, whale

"-aid" / "-ade" words:
aid, braid, laid, maid, paid, raid, afraid, *aide, *stayed, *grayed, *suede

blade, fade, grade, jade, made, shade, spade, trade, wade

"-ed" / "-ead" words
bed, bled, bred, fed, fled, led, red, shed, shred, Ted, wed

bread, dead, dread, lead, read, head, spread, thread, tread, *said

Here are three examples of a child's rhymes using **ail/ale**, **aid/ade**, and **ed/ead**:

> <u>Gail</u> got <u>mail</u> about a <u>whale</u>. It was <u>pale</u> and <u>frail</u> with a <u>tail</u>.
> She will <u>nail</u> the <u>mail</u> to the <u>rail</u> and put the <u>whale</u> up for <u>sale</u>.

> The <u>maid</u> with the <u>braid</u> got <u>paid</u>.
> She was <u>afraid</u> she would <u>fade</u> if not in the <u>shade</u>.

> Ted and Fred led Mr. Ned to the bed in the red shed. Ted bled while he was sledding on the shiny red sled, that he found on the bed in the red shed. Fred got sick and had to go to the bed in the creepy shed. "I don't like it in this creepy old shed in the small little bed," Ned said. Ted and Mr. Ned were having fun riding on the sled. But Ned was still in bed.

APPLYING STRATEGIES WHEN READING AND WRITING
(ASSESSING PROGRESS)

Good assessment is an ongoing activity. Teachers watch their children in a variety of reading and writing situations and notice what strategies they are using and what they need to move them forward. Many teachers designate a fifth of their children to each day of the week. On Monday, their clipboard contains the anecdotal record sheets for the "Monday children"; the teachers write down what they notice about the reading and writing strategies these Monday children are using. At the end of Monday, they file away the Monday sheets and attach to their clipboards the record sheet for the Tuesday children. This procedure makes the notion of anecdotal records workable and also assures that no child gets "lost in the shuffle" because each child gets "noticed" on a weekly schedule.

These ongoing observations of children let us know what many children are ready to learn. They also remind us what nudges particular children need. In addition, it is also good from time to time to stop and assess progress in a more systematic way. For many teachers, **the half-way point in second grade is a good time to do some more systematic assessment.** In spite of the fact that this book is primarily about how to teach phonics and spelling strategies in second grade, we can only assess these strategies by looking at their actual reading and writing. **Remembering the principle, "What they don't use, they don't have!" we assess their decoding and spelling as they are actually reading and writing.**

Observing Word Strategies In Reading

In observing children's reading, teachers can look at the errors or miscues that children make and determine what word identification strategies they are using. Good readers will self-correct many of their miscues. This usually indicates that they are using context to check that what they are reading makes sense. **Successful self-correction is an excellent indicator that the reader is using all three cueing systems—meaning (semantic), sounding-like language (syntactic) and letter-sound knowledge (graphophonic)—successfully.** Some readers tend to overuse context; their miscues make sense but don't have most of the letter-sound relationships of the original word. Others overuse letter-sound knowledge. Their miscues look and sound a lot like the original words but they don't make any sense. By observing children's reading, we can determine what strategies they are using and what kind of instructional activities we might provide for them.

To look at children's word strategies while reading, we first must have something for them to read in which they make some errors—but not too many. This level is generally referred to as "instructional level"—the level of a book or story in which the child correctly identifies at least 90-95 percent of the words and has adequate comprehension of what was read. The text the child is reading should be something the child has not read before. Although the child may read more than 100 words, the first 100 words are generally used for analysis.

Teachers use a variety of materials to do this assessment—depending on what is available and what the school system requires. Some teachers use passages contained in the assessment package that accompanies many basal reading series. Other teachers/schools have designated certain "real" books as benchmark books. They don't use these books for instruction but only for assessment purposes. They decide which book first graders could read at the 90-95% word identification accuracy level early in the year and call this pre-primer level. Another book, which most could read half way through the year, represents primer difficulty level. A third book is selected as end of first-grade level. **They choose two second-grade books, one for early in the year, one for later in the year.** They also choose a book or books for each grade level. In schools where Reading Recovery is used, some first- and second-grade teachers use books designated by Reading Recovery scoring to be at particular levels. Finally, some teachers use a published Informal Reading Inventory that contains graded passages beginning at preprimer level and going through eighth grade.

Regardless of what you use, the procedures are the same.

1. You have the child read the text you think will be at the instructional level. This text should be a text the child has **not** had a chance to read previously.

2. The child should be told that you cannot help him or her while reading. When they get to a word they don't know, they should do the best they can to figure it out because you can't tell them any words.

3. Also, tell them that they should think about what they are reading because after they have read, they will be asked to retell in their own words what the text was about.

As the child reads, we record what they read using procedures adapted from Marie Clay's (1993) **system for taking a Running Record.** If we have made a copy of the text (or if we are using a passage from a basal assessment or an Informal Reading Inventory), we mark right on the passage. If not, we simply record on a sheet of paper. Here are the recordings for one child on one passage. To show that it can be done either way, we have shown the record on a copy of the passage and on a Running Record sheet. (Of course you would only need to record it one way or the other!)

Storytellers, by Diana Yurkovic. (Shortland Publications, 1998).

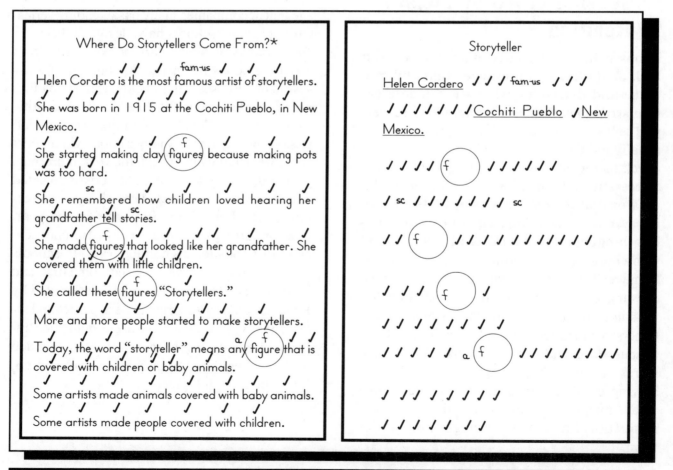

As you can tell from the sample, we use a simple marking system and we only score the first 100 words (even though the passage read might be somewhat longer.)

Put a check mark over each word read correctly.

✓
funny

If the child misreads a word (slick for slippery) write the error above the word.

slick
slippery

If the child leaves a word out, circle that word.

What's that (all) about

If the child self-corrects, write **SC** above it. **SC** words are counted as correct.

If the child makes the same error more than once, only count it one time.

After the child has read the passage, have the child close the book (or take the passage away). Ask the child to tell what the text was about. Ask questions needed to determine if the child understood at least 70-80% of the information read.

In our example, the class was talking and reading about storytellers. Neither the teacher nor the class had read this book. The teacher told the class that this was about Helen Cordero from the Cochiti Pueblo in New Mexico. The children then began to read the passage. This child misread or left out four words, giving that child a word identification accuracy rate of 96%. Comprehension was adequate. This passage appears to be at the instructional level of the child since the teacher did not count the names and places she gave them. She did not help with any other words. We can now analyze the child's errors and self-corrections to determine what word strategies the child is actually using.

(If we wanted to determine the highest level at which this child could read, we would need to have the child continue reading higher and higher passages until word identification accuracy drops below the 90-95% level or comprehension falls below the 70-80% level.)

Looking at the words read correctly, errors and self-corrections, we know that:

- The child is developing a store of high-frequency words since *Word Wall* words are being read correctly (**was, because, children, made, them, little, more, people**, and **making**).

- The child is cross-checking meaning and letter sounds since the self-corrections were probably triggered by the meaning of the words in the sentence made after the initial error (**remembered, stories**).

- The child is using initial letter knowledge since the three words misread all began with the correct letters ("fam-us" for **famous**, "a" for **any**, and the child made the correct beginning sound each time they got to the word **figure** or **figures**).

- The child knows compound words (**grandfather, storyteller**).

- The child is unsure about what to do with big words since the two words omitted were both polysyllabic words (**figure, figures**).

Since this passage was determined by this teacher to be "about right" for second grade, we can determine that at this level, the child is applying what he knows about sight words, meaning and letter-sounds while reading.

Imagine, however, that on this passage, the child being assessed had only made one error—giving him a word identification accuracy rate of 99%—and had had adequate comprehension. We would, of course, be pleased because this passage is "about right" for most children in the middle of second-grade. The child being assessed is a better than average reader. But, what can we tell about that child's decoding? We might just decide that this child is moving along fine, and that we don't need to know anymore. If we did feel the need to assess the child's decoding, however, we would need to find a passage for him in which his word identification accuracy was in the 90-95% range so that we could see what strategies are used for decoding unknown words.

On the other hand, imagine that the child makes 15 errors on this middle-of-second-grade passage. When a child is making that many errors, it is impossible to cross-check meaning and letter sounds because so much of the meaning is missing in all the words left out or miscalled. We can't make judgments about the child's decoding-while-reading abilities until we have the child reading a passage at the instructional level. We need to find a text where the child's word-identification accuracy is at the 90-95% level with 70-80% comprehension. Then we can analyze the errors on that passage.

OBSERVING WORD STRATEGIES IN WRITING

Writing samples also show growth in word knowledge. Because writing results in a visible, external product, it is easier to determine what they are actually using. By looking at two or three writing samples done a month or more apart, progress in word development is easy to determine. In looking at their writing sample to determine their level of word knowledge, **we want to look at their spelling of high-frequency words and their attempts at spelling less-frequent words.** Here is a sample written by one second grader. **Highlighted words are all on the *Word Wall*. The words in boxes were not on the *Word Wall* but were displayed on theme boards or in other places in the room. The remaining words are words the child spelled as best he could. (Circled words are words the child circled which he believes are not spelled correctly.)** What can we tell about her developing word knowledge by looking at this sample?

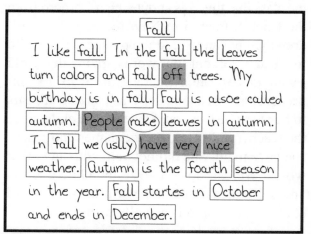

First, we notice that all the *Word Wall* words are spelled correctly. The fact that all the boxed words are also spelled correctly shows that this child knows how to use the print in the room to help her spell words.

Next, we look at how the child is spelling words not apt to be known by a second grader and not readily available in the room. This child spelled **also** as **alsoe**, and **usually** as **uslly**.

These are very good attempts at spelling and show that the child is able to hear sounds in words and knows what letters usually represent those sounds.

The next sample is taken from a another second grader. Only a few words (underlined) are misspelled, and these incorrect spellings show a sophisticated understanding of letters, sounds, and spelling patterns.

C.J. and I

C.J. and I are friends. We play together. We have fun. We like football. He wants to play on the Titins. He want to be linebacker. I am Quarterback. He likes the Carolina Panthers and Wake Forest Demind Decins. We like to ride bikes.

Finally, we have included a writing sample from a child who is still struggling with words and spelling. The words on the wall (highlighted here) are not spelled correctly in his first draft. Using the *Word Wall* would help this child. The only word seen in the room, which was correctly spelled, was his teacher's name. Although this child's word knowledge is not where you might expect the average second grader to be at this point in the year, almost all the words are decipherable by an experienced reader of children's spelling attempts.

I lik Mrs Boger
She is vuere nise sum tims
She is nise unuf to let us plae
up win it ranes
the end
I love you Mrs. Boger.

In addition to writings on self-selected topics, many schools collect focused writing samples and look at these to determine growth in writing ability and word knowledge. A focused writing sample collected for assessment purposes should have a topic specified about which most children have good general knowledge. Children should write on this topic with no assistance from the teacher or any other child. Some examples of topics used in primary classrooms include:

- My Friend
- Second Grade
- My Favorite Book
- My Favorite Author

Many schools have the child write about the same topic at several different points in time—May of Kindergarten, January and May of First Grade, January and May of Second grade, for example. These topic-focused, non-assisted first drafts are then compared to determine an individual child's writing growth. In addition we gather a great deal of valuable information about how the child writes—sentence sense, topic sense, word choice, writing conventions, etc. These samples yield valuable information about the child's developing word knowledge.

Sample #1   **George**

My Friends

Trey and Stephanie Trey and Stephanie is my best friend. Sometimes thay play with me out side. Thay help Sometime with my eraly bird work. I love Trey and Stephanie. Thay love me to.

Sample #2   **Ashley**

My Friend
My Friends name is Stephanie. She is a nice person. I like her. She is the best silly girl at school. She is kind to me. I like her very much! I sit bye Stephanie. She helped me on Thursday with the penquin picture. Her bestfriends name is Katy, Kristen, and Ashley. She is crazy. Now I sit with Stephanie. Every time I go to school I sit with her.

Sample #3   **Kelsy**

Katherine
I want to tell you about Katherine. Katherine is my best friend. She has brown hair and her eye color is hasal. Katherine has four pets, the are two dogs a cat, and a hamster. She goes to her dad's house on Friday. Her fairt food is fried okra and her favirt drink is grape colade. The animals she likes best are a chimack and a rabbit. Katherine is 7½ years old, and her birthday is Decmber 19th. Her favirt place to go is the mall. The best things Katherine likes about school are math and running the track. Katherine is a Browny Scout. Her best friend is Rachle. Rachle lives in Ohio. She has very nice illustashins. When Katherine grows up she want's to work at the bank. Her favirit show to watch is Figure it out, and her favirit book is Nobody's Mother is in Second Grade. She has one brother and she has two sister's. She lives in a two stoie house and has an atick and a basement. She has published two books at school. Her favirit restrant to eat at is Quinsy's. These are some thigs I know about Katherine.

OBSERVING WORD STRATEGIES FOR SPELLING UNKNOWN WORDS

Finally, there is one more quick and simple measure we like to use halfway through second grade to determine how children are developing their word knowledge. Making sure that each child cannot see what others are writing, **we dictate ten words to them which we don't expect them to be able to spell. Then, we analyze their attempts. Teachers use a variety of words, the major criterion being that these words are not and have not been available in the room, and that they show a variety of different patterns. Many teachers use the ten words suggested by Gentry and Gillet on their Developmental Spelling Test** (1993):

- monster
- united
- dress
- bottom
- hiked
- human
- eagle
- closed
- bumped
- type

(If your children like to write about monsters and thus have learned to spell monster, you might substitute another word, perhaps **blister** or **mountain**.)

Once children have spelled these words as best they can, Gentry and Gillet suggest analyzing their spelling using the following stages:

The Precommunicative Stage: Spelling at this stage contains scribbles, circles, and lines with a few letters thrown in at random. These letters usually are just there and any connection between these letters and the words they are thinking is pure coincidence.

The Semiphonetic Stage: The second stage can be seen when words begin to be represented by a letter or two. The word **monster** may be written with just an **m** or an **mr** or an **mtr**. Type might be written with just a **t** or **tp**. This stage indicates that the child is beginning to understand letter-sound relationships and knows the consonant letters which represent some sounds.

The Phonetic Stage: In the third stage, vowels appear—not necessarily always the right vowels but vowels are used and most sounds are represented by at least one letter. Phonetic spelling of **monster** might include **munstr** and **mostr**. **Type** will probably be spelled **tip**. You can usually tell when a child is in the phonetic stage because you can read most of what children in this stage write.

The Transitional Stage: In this stage all sounds are represented and the spelling is usually a possible English spelling, just not necessarily the correct spelling. **Monster** in this stage might be spelled **monstir** or **monstur**. **Type** is probably spelled **tipe**.

The Conventional Stage: Finally, the child reaches the stage of conventional spelling in which most words which a child at that grade level could be expected to spell correctly are spelled correctly.

Of course, **children's spelling of different words will indicate different stages.** Most second graders are beyond the Precommunicative and Prephonemic Stages. We have been working in second grade to get them beyond the Phonetic Stage. The important thing is not which stage they are in but how they are growing. Put the sample away, along with writing samples and running records, and use them to compare how they do on the very same tasks toward the end of the year.

Children come to us on all different literacy and word levels, and they develop their literacy and word abilities at different rates. "Grade level" means "average." They aren't now and never will be—and we shouldn't want them all to be!—average! What we can expect (and should document) is growth. Children come to us multilevel. Our instruction and assessment cannot deny this truth!

February is here—that short but busy month. Winter is still with us; cold and storms are still expected in many parts of the country. Some places have "winter vacation" so that families can enjoy the snow or escape and go to warmer climates. Some schools close when it snows while others are so used to the snow that, unless there is a blizzard, they keep school open! Still other parts of the country are warm and children have heard of snow but have not seen it.

There are many things to talk about in second grade at school—Valentine's Day (LOVE), Dental Health Month, Washington's Birthday/Lincoln's Birthday. Now both are celebrated on President's Day, but many traditional teachers still give them each their due on their February birthdays. This seems like a lot to do along with other themes that may be studied, such as animals in the winter. How do you get it all done in such a short month? Routine! Keep reading and writing about these topics as you do the Four Blocks every day. Choose books to read that will help your children learn about these topics. Model the writing of stories about these topics. Share what you know and how you learned about them. Use interesting words and activities to help your children learn more about words.

CALENDAR						
	1	2	3	4	5	
6	7	8	9	10	11	12
13	14	15	16	17	18	19
20	21	22	23	24	25	26
27	28	29	30	31		

MONTH AT A GLANCE

By the end of February, you will have reviewed the following:

- Two new *On-the-Back* activities:

  1. Writing sentences with *Word Wall* and theme words

  2. Endings where you have to drop the "e," double the consonant, or change "y" to "i" before adding the ending

- *Guess the Covered Word* with a continued emphasis on 2 and 3 letter blends

- *Making Words* with an emphasis on 2 and 3-letter blends, patterns, and endings

- *Reading/Writing Rhymes* with more than one spelling pattern (**eet/eat**)

- Reminders to use before and after reading and writing

WORD WALL

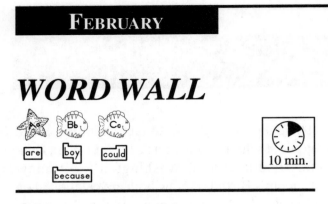

10 min.

ON-THE-BACK ACTIVITIES
(FOCUSING ON WORDS IN SENTENCES)

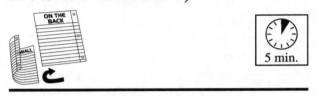

5 min.

Continue to add words to your *Word Wall* and make sure your students are using them when they are writing, even in their first drafts. We want these words to be written right so they won't be practiced wrong! You will probably have a February holiday board which in addition to pictures contains words such as: **Valentine's Day, valentines, cards, party, George Washington, Abraham Lincoln, president,** etc. Some of your second graders will want to add these words to their pictionaries. Continue to do activities *On-the-Back* of the *Word Wall* paper to extend the word knowledge of all the students.

One *On-the-Back* activity will help children remember to use the theme board just as they use the *Word Wall* when writing. **Say two simple sentences with *Word Wall* words and theme words in each one. The children write these on the back, using the *Word Wall* and theme board to help them.** Some sentences you could use this month are:

> I will **write** my **name** on my **valentines.**
>
> I got **cards** for my **friends.**

> Who was **George Washington?**
>
> He was the **first president.**

Ending—Drop the "e" before adding the ending

Another *On-the-Back* activity you might want to introduce this month is how to spell *Word-Wall* words with endings where you have to drop the "e" before adding the ending. Imagine that the five *Word Wall* words you called out for them to locate, clap or cheer for, and write were:

make	phone	ride	skate	write

Have them turn their papers over and say something like:

"Today we are going to work on how to spell these *Word Wall* words when they need an ending. I will say some sentences that some of you might write, and you listen for the *Word Wall* word that has had an ending added:

I am **making** cookies after school.

I was **phoning** my friend when the line went dead.

Tim was **riding** his new bike.

I like **skating** with my friends.

David is good at **writing** stories."

After each sentence, the children identify the *Word Wall* word and the ending. They decide how to spell it, and write it on their papers. In this activity you need to drop the "e" before adding "ing." Second graders need to learn and review this concept. **On this day, you focus on just one ending.** On another day, you could also include some words that needed to have the y changed to i, or a letter doubled, before the ending is added. This additional information about spelling words with a variety of endings and spelling changes really moves the accelerated learners along in their writing ability. **At least one day each week, make sure the five words you call can have endings added to them. For the *On-the-Back* activity, tell them sentences that contain one of the *Word Wall* words with s, ed, er or ing added to it. They have to decide what the *Word Wall* word is and how to spell it with its ending. This may be a good time to start including some words that need to have the e dropped before adding *ing*. Before allowing anyone to write the word, be sure to have the children tell you that they must drop the e before adding *ing* so that all children will have the words correctly spelled.**

Some other words you might want to use for *On-the-Back* activities help children to learn when to double the consonant and when not to:

stopping, stopped, joker, joked, phoned, having, tripping, tripped, stopping, stopped, skater, skated, writer, bugging, bugged, quitting, and quitter.

GUESS THE COVERED WORD

Guess the covered word.

15 min.

The year is more than half over, and you might be tempted to stop doing *Guess The Covered Word* activities because many of your children know most of the beginning sounds in words. However, children don't know something until they use it in their reading and writing. *Guess the Covered Word* focuses the children's attention on ALL the letters up to the vowel—not just the first one. **In addition, *Guess the Covered Word* is the activity in which we teach and remind children that guessing based only on the first letters—or only on how long the word is—or only on what makes sense—won't help you figure out many words in your reading. Guessing the word when you take all three cues—beginning letters up to the vowel, the length of the word, and what makes sense—will give you the word more often than not.** In spite of all our helpful *On-the-Back* rhyming activities, sorting and transferring during *Making Words,* and other activities, **there are children who never get very good at figuring out the vowel part of the word. These children can become very good readers, however, if they can learn to cross check beginning letters, length, and meaning.**

Continue with *Guess the Covered Word:*

- until almost all your children represent almost all the beginning letters correctly in their invented spelling

- until they make guesses for unknown words during writing that begin with all the right letters

- word guesses are about the right length

- word guesses make sense

Activities such as *Guess the Covered Word* help children do these things. For those who have become good decoders and who think automatically, they still enjoy the "game" because it does not take long, and they are thinking and guessing along with the other students. All students like activities where they are actively involved. Those accelerated students probably come up with the accurate guess as soon as they see the beginning letter(s) for they have already used context to get close. They are able to use context, beginning sound, and word length. They are usually right with their guesses, and that is satisfying to them. One day every week or two, they should find sentences such as these on the board. Note that the word to be guessed is covered with two self-adhesive notes and that the self-adhesive notes are cut to reveal the length of the word. The first self-adhesive note covers all the letters up to the vowel. Using themes and seasonal words along with the students' names makes this activity more fun.

Remember that children's natural tendency seems to be to only consider the first letter. A child who guesses **subway**, when the "sc" of **scooter** or the "sl" of **sled** has been revealed, should be told: "That's a good guess for the 's,' and it makes sense because you can ride on the **subway**, but **subway** does not have an 'sc.' If it did, it wouldn't be a **subway**, it would be a **scubway**!" Here are some *Guess the Covered Word* activities for February.

Valentine's Day

Jose gives **candy** on Valentine's Day.

Chocolate candy is Linda's favorite.

Some cupcakes have **hearts** on them.

Rolando gets **cards** from his friends.

John likes to write **poem**s in his valentines.

President's Day

Washington lived long ago.

He never told a **lie.**

Lincoln was honest too.

He had a **beard.**

We remember them on their **birthdays.**

When Winter Comes

Bears hibernate and so do **snakes.**

Geese fly south for the winter.

Deer search for food in the **snow.**

Rabbits make **footprints** in the snow.

Michelle will help the animals by leaving **crumbs** outside.

Winter Fun

Carlos likes to ride on the **snowplow.**

Ryan rides on his **sled** down big hills.

Suzanne likes to **skate** in the winter.

Rusty likes to play his **trumpet.**

This winter, Molly learned to **ski.**

MAKING WORDS

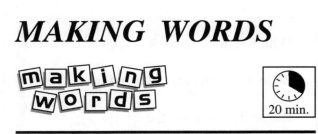

⏱ 20 min.

In most second grades in February, we no longer need to sort for single initial letters, since almost all children use these correctly to decode words while reading and to spell words while writing. If this is not true of your class, continue to sort first for beginning letters. Notice that you use the same letter to make them, and you say the same sound when you read them. **We do, however, sort when we have two or more words such as *true* and *trust*, which begin with two or more letters that have the same sound. We also sort out words with endings. When we have plurals or the same ending (*seeder/ feeder*) we put these together.** If we just have two such as **feed** and **feeder**, we pull those out and talk about how they both have the word **feed**, and that a feeder is the person or thing that **feeds** someone or something. **We sort beginning letters and endings first and end with the words sorted according to rhymes so that we can use the spelling patterns in these rhymes to read and spell some transfer words.**

Here are some particularly apt February (Animals in Winter) *Making Words* lessons that continue the **focus on changing letters around to make new words, two- and three-letter blends, and adding "s" to make a word plural.** Watch to see if the two- and three-letter words are becoming automatic for your students who were struggling at the beginning of the year. See if students who had to say the word in order to spell the word are now spelling them automatically. Students whose word knowledge is improving will use different strategies to spell the words. Manipulating the little letter cards helps some students "see" how words work.

Secret Word: animals
Letters: a, a, i, l, m, n, s
Make: is, as, am, an, man, aim, ail, mail, nail, sail, slam, slim, snail, salami, animals
Sort: sl-, –am, –ail, –an
Transfer Words: scram, tram, van, trail

Secret Word: hibernate
Letters: a, e, e, i, b, h, n, r, t
Make: be, bee, eat/ate, her, hen, Ben, been, beet, beat, heat/hate, Nate/neat, tree, intern, hibernate
Sort: Names, beet-beat (homophones), –ee, –eat, –en,–ate
Transfer: free, cheat, treat, when, plate

Secret Word: raccoon
Letters: a, o, o, c, c, n, r
Make: on, or, an, ran, can, car/arc, oar, corn, acorn, cocoa, croon, raccoon
Sort: –an, –oon, –orn
Transfer: bran, horn, thorn, spoon

Secret Word: beavers
Letters: a, e, e, b, r, s, v
Make: be, bee, are/ear, bear/bare, bars, save/vase, verb, bears, brave, erase, verse, serve, beavers
Sort: plurals, –ave, –ase
Transfer: crave, slave, chase, chases

Secret Word: turtles
Letters: e, u, l, r, s, t, t
Make: us, use, let, set, rut, rust, rest, test, true, user, rule, rules, trust/strut, result, turtles
Sort: tr, plurals, –et, –ust, –ut
Transfer: vet, yet, crust, shut

Secret Word: feeders
Letters: e, e, e, d, f, r, s
Make: see, fee, fed, red, deer, seed, feed, fees, free, freed, feeder, seeder, feeders
Sort: f-, fr-, plurals, ending "er", –ed, –eed, -ee
Transfer: three, tweed, bleed, bleeder

Secret Word: snakes
Letters: a, e, k, n, s, s
Make: an, as, ask, Ken, sea, seas, asks, sank, sake, snake/ sneak, snakes
Sort: s-, sn-, plurals, –ake
Transfer: shake, flake, flakes, brakes

Secret Word: amazing
Letters: a, a, i, g, m, n, z
Make: in, an, am, aim, man, nag, zag, zing, gain, main, mania, again, amazing
Sort: –an, –ain, –ag
Transfer: clan, Spain, brain, brag

READING/ WRITING RHYMES

READING & WRITING

sand
stand
hand

mice
twice
nice

RHYMES

20 min.

Before beginning your *Reading/Writing Rhymes* lessons this month, **ask students how they use what they learn in *Reading/Writing Rhymes* when they are reading and writing. Get them to explain that when you come to a word you do not recognize immediately while reading, you can often figure it out by thinking of a rhyming word you do know. These rhyming words you know also help you with the last chunk of many longer words. Get them to understand that good spellers spell by patterns and that rhyming words often have the same spelling pattern.**

Next, explain that many rhyming words can be spelled with two common patterns, as we saw last month and will continue to work with this month. How do we know which one to use? We need to have seen the words several times so that we know what looks right. For this month, we will work with three such patterns: **eat/eet, ead/eet,** and **ite/ight.** When you make a chart write both patterns. Words that do not fit either pattern but rhyme go in the * column. We will start with **ide** and **ied** which rhyme but have different spelling patterns.

First we make our chart.

"__ide" / "__ied" chart

__ide	__ied
__ide	__ied
__ide	__ied
__ide	__ied
__ide	__ied
__ide	__ied
__ide	__ied
__ide	__ied
__ide	__ied

Then, we pass out the onset deck, the 50 beginning letters and sounds. The children come up with the letters that they think make rhyming words. The teacher decides which letters to write under the **ide** and **ied** spelling patterns on the chart. These letters will make words. Sometimes (like **pride** and **pried**) they go with both spelling patterns. The teacher explains this and gives a sentence for each. When we are finished, our chart looks like this:

"__ide" / "__ied" chart

__ide	__ied
bride	cried
chide	fried
glide	lied
hide	pried
pride	tried
ride	*sighed
side	
slide	
stride	
tide	
wide	
beside	
inside	
outside	

Next, we make up a silly rhyme with the children:

> The **bride** will **ride inside** to **hide**.
>
> The **guide** stepped **outside** as she **cried** and **lied**.

Finally, the children make up their own rhymes writing them by themselves or with a partner. We have seen children write one line each, alternating lines with their partner; these have been some of the best rhymes written!

Here are other patterns to work on this month. Remember to use just one chart for the two spelling patterns with the same rhyming sounds.

"-eat" / "-eet" words

beat, bleat, cheat, eat, neat, feat, heat, meat, pleat, seat, treat, wheat

beet, feet, fleet, greet, meet, sheet, sleet, street, sweet, tweet

"-ead" / "-eed" words

bead, knead, lead, plead, read

bleed, breed, deed, feed, reed, freed, greed, heed, need, seed, speed, steed

"-ite" / "-ight" words

bite, cit, site, kite, quite, spite, sprite, trite, white, write

blight, sight, bright, Dwight, fight, flight, fright, knight, light, might, night, plight, sight, tight

APPLYING STRATEGIES WHEN READING AND WRITING

In any classroom the majority of the time should be devoted to actual reading and writing. The decoding and spelling strategies described here will only be helpful to students if they are reading and writing everyday and beginning to employ these strategies as they read and write. Here are some "reminders" that teachers use for their students as they begin a reading or writing activity.

Before reading:

"When we read, we come to words that we have heard but have never seen before in print. When you come to an unfamiliar word, stop and say all the letters in that word. Don't try to sound out each letter, just spell the word to yourself, naming all the letters. If you can come up with a word, try it out and see if it makes sense. Remember that "guessing" a word based on meaning, or just on the first letters, or on how long or short the word is, won't work very well. But when you combine all three as we do in *Guess the Covered Word* lessons, you can make a good guess if the word is one you have heard before."

After Reading:

Ask students for examples of words they figured out by saying all the letters and looking in their word stores for words with similar patterns or by using meaning and all the beginning letters and word length. You may want to give them a self-adhesive note as they begin to read and ask them to write down one word they figured out for themselves. Remember second graders often know more than they use when reading and writing.

Before Writing:

"As you are writing, concentrate on what you are trying to say—the meaning or the message. **When you finish writing, but before putting your piece away for the day,** reread it, looking for any *Word Wall* words that you spelled incorrectly. Correct these. Look for other words you spelled as best you could but which don't look right to you. Do you know a rhyming word that might have the same spelling pattern? Write it that way and see if it looks right."

After Writing:

Ask students to come up with examples of *Word Wall* words they fixed. Ask them to share examples of words that didn't look right and for which they tried a different spelling pattern. Praise their efforts to monitor their spelling and apply what they are learning.

MARCH

Whether March comes in like a lion or a lamb, spring will soon be here. March is magic with kites flying, leprechauns leaping, and pots of gold shimmering. Children like March winds turning their clothes inside out as they walk to school. The last of the cold weather will soon be just a memory. Spring weather is greeted with enthusiasm. Light jackets and longer days are a welcome relief after winter. Children and their families have fun with kites, and as their kites soar, so do their spirits—they can read, they can write, they can fly!

Children at this age can have a good attitude if we let them know they are making progress—and they should be! Green is the color of March and spring and leprechauns. Don't let those little (getting bigger) leprechauns trick you this month—they can read and write! Let them prove it to you as you become their cheerleader and celebrate their growing knowledge.

MONTH AT A GLANCE

By the end of March, you will have reviewed the following:

1. *Word Wall On-the-Back* activities where you combine rhyming words and endings

2. *Guess the Covered Word* lessons that use a paragraph not just sentences

3. *Making Words* that emphasize book/writing words, beginning letter clusters, plurals, homophones, and changing letters around to make new words

4. *Reading/Writing Rhymes* with **o** vowel patterns

5. *Using Words You Know* as a strategy to read and write unknown, or less familiar, one-syllable and two-syllable words

WORD WALL

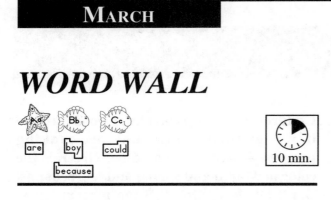

10 min.

ON-THE-BACK ACTIVITIES
(REVIEWING ENDINGS AND RHYMING WORDS)

5 min.

Your *Word Wall* will probably have 100 words or more by the end of this month. The helpfulness of having this many high-frequency words instantly available to them should be obvious by the fluency with which they are writing. Remember that if you invest an extra 2-3 minutes in an *On-the Back* activity, you can greatly increase the utility of the words displayed on your wall, achieve some additional handwriting practice, and not waste the back of that half-sheet of paper!

Continue to practice writing *Word Wall* words with *s*, *ed*, and *ing* and, if spelling changes are needed, don't hesitate to use that word. As long as you tell them about the spelling change before they write it, they can all spell it correctly. **Some of your fast word learners will learn that you need to drop the *e* when you add *ing* to *write, have, make, ride,* etc. and double the *p* when you add *ing* to *stop* or *trip*.**

When adding a new word such as snap to the wall, you have the perfect opportunity to remind them that some words can help them spell lots of other words. **This month, combine rhyme and endings for some of your words. After calling out five words and self-correcting them, have the children turn over their papers and listen for the word that rhymes with snap in each sentence.**

Next, they write these words on the back of their paper. In March, you could use these sentences:

1. We will **clap** when the kite is up in the air.

2. The **map** showed where the pot of gold was hidden.

3. The **trap** was set to catch a leprechaun.

4. The **strap** would hold him tight.

5. The **kite** flapped in the breeze.

GUESS THE COVERED WORD

Guess the covered word.

20 min.

Remember to provide practice with cross-checking by occasionally giving students some sentences or a paragraph in which they have to guess some words—first with no letters showing and then with all the letters up to the vowel. **This month we will use a paragraph to *Guess the Covered Word* in each sentence.** You write the paragraph just as you did the sentences, covering the target word with two self-adhesive notes—one for the beginning letter(s) and one for the rest of the word you are guessing. **Students should be getting good at using meaning, beginning letters, and word length to figure out words.** Here is an example appropriate for March:

March

Spring begins in March. It gets windy in March. Sometimes I wear a sweatshirt to play outside. I can ride a bicycle. I can play with my pet. Some people fly kites high up in the clouds. The wind catches the kite and it soars. The wind blows your clothes. In March, I like to stay outside.

MAKING WORDS

making words

⏱ 20 min.

In addition to some easy lessons like "spring," you could do some March lessons using the words **Patrick** and **leprechaun**. Since we have done these words in other books, we want to give you some "new" lessons to focus on writing (and illustrating) words this month: writers, author, artists, painter, pictures, notebook, and journal. It is good to continue to do some easier lessons as the year moves along as well as some more complex ones. Some of your children are just beginning to get a sense of how words work and it is a great ego-booster for the students if they can figure out the "secret word" occasionally. They are also ready to understand that many words sound the same and have different spellings. The children have encountered these words on the Word Wall and in *Reading/Writing Rhymes*. We can also sort for them during *Making Words*. Several of the lessons for March are set up to do just that. On the other hand, it is also good to have an occasional tricky lesson— particularly one planned by a leprechaun!

Secret Word: journal
Letters: a, o, u, j, l, n, r
Make: or, on, an, Jan, ran, run, nor, jar, our, oar, loan, oral, lunar, journal
Sort: j-, related words (ran/run), –or, –an
Transfer: for, span, Stan, scan

Secret Word: notebook
Letters: e, o, o, o, b, k, n, t
Make: be, on, to, ton/not, knot, note, boot, book, took, nook, token, notebook
Sort: not/knot (homophones), compound words (notebook), –ot, –ook
Transfer: slot, plot, shook, brook

Secret Word: author
Letters: a, o, u, h, t, r
Make: at, or, our, out, art/tar/rat, rot, hot, hat, hut, hurt, hour, auto, author
Sort: our/hour (homophones), –at, –ot
Transfer: scat, splat, blot, spot

Secret Word: artists
Letters: a, i, r, s, s, t, t
Make: is, as, it, at, sat, rat/art, air, sit, sir, stir, star, tart, tarts, stars, stair, stairs, artists
Sort: plurals, –it, –at, –art, –ar, –air
Transfer: splat, smart, jar, chairs

Secret Word: painter
Letters: a, e, i, n, p, r, t
Make: it, at, art/rat/tar, par, pat/tap, tip/pit, rip, pen, pan, pant, part, rain, pain, paint, painter
Sort: –at, –ar, –it, –art, –ain
Transfer: slat, split, start, stain

Secret Word: pictures
Letters: e, i, u, c, p, r, s, t
Make: is, sip, sit, set, pet, pie, tie, ice, rice, price, purse, crisp, crust, cruise, pictures
Sort: cr-, –et, –e
Transfer: vet, lie, spice, twice

Secret Word: writers
Letters: e, i, r, r, s, t, w
Make: it, we, wet, wit, sit, set, sew, tie, tire, wire, west, rest, tires, wires, write, writers
Sort: plurals, –et,–it, –est, –ire
Transfer: yet, fire, guest, guests

Secret Word: Patrick
Letters: a, i, c, k, p, r, t
Make: at, it, cap, tap, rap, part, cart, pack, tack, rack, pick, tick, trip, trap, trick, Patrick
Sort: t-, tr-, –ap, –ack, –art
Transfer: slap, clap, stack, snack

Secret Word: leprechaun
Letters: a, e, e, u, c, h, l, n, p, r (This is the lesson left by a leprechaun.)
Make: he, her, heel, heal, real, reel, each, chap, clap, clean, peach/cheap, lunch, preach, leprechaun
Sort: cl-, ch-, heel-heal, reel-real (homophones), –ap, –eel, –eal, –each
Transfer: scrap, strap, reach, bleach

READING/ WRITING RHYMES

⏱ 20 min.

This month we will work on some *o* vowel patterns. The *old, ook,* and *oom* patterns were chosen because they are familiar to the children and used frequently when reading and writing. Write your pattern 10-12 times on a chart and pass out the onset deck of cards to your children. Some words you can make with this pattern are:

bold	mold	*bowled
cold	old	*polled
fold	sold	*rolled
gold	scold	*strolled
hold	told	

Now, write a silly rhyme with the children.

One **cold, bold** day I **sold** my **gold.** Don't **scold!**

I was **told** my **gold** had **mold** and was **old.**

Finally, let the children have fun writing their own rhymes. When they finish, let some of the children share their rhymes with the class. You will see that second-grade children are quite good at *Reading/Writing Rhymes*.

These are words you can write with the **ook** and **oom** patterns.

"-ook" words

book, cook, hook, look, nook, took, brook, shook, mistook, unhook

---

"-oom" words

boom, bloom, broom, doom, gloom, groom, loom, room, zoom, bathroom, *fume, *plume, *tomb

---

The other patterns chosen for this month are **oke/oak** and **oat/ote.** Each of these rhymes can be represented by two spelling patterns. Sometimes one of the patterns does not generate many words (**oak**) but you still put it on one chart with the **oke** words (**oke/oak**).

"-oke" / "-oak" words

broke, choke, joke, poke, smoke, spoke, troke, woke, awoke, slowpoke

croak, soak, oak, *folk

"-oat" / "-ote" words

boat, coat, float, goat, gloat, throat, afloat

dote, note, quote, tote, vote, wrote, devote, remote, rewrote

---

USING WORDS YOU KNOW

Using Words You Know
tan... plan

15 min.

Using Words You Know **is an activity that helps students see that you can use what you know to figure out what you do not know.** For example, second-grade students know the color words: **red**, **green**, **brown**, and **black**.

1. Display the color words on the board or a chart, and talk about the words.

2. Identify the spelling patterns (**ed, ee, own,** and **ack**).

3. Have the students make 4 columns on their paper. Head these with the color words and underline the spelling patterns.

4. **Show them some one-syllable words written on index cards. Have them write these words under the word with the same pattern and then use the rhyme to pronounce the words. End with a word with two syllables, so the children can see how to chunk words and use this knowledge for bigger words.**

5. **Say some one-syllable words and have the children decide how to spell them by deciding which word they rhyme with. Then, say some two-syllable words. See if they can write them using the spelling pattern in the last syllable, and familiar words or word parts (prefixes), to help them decide on the spelling.**

Words you know:

red   green   brown   black

Words to read:

queen	crown	knack	shed
attack	touchdown	between	coed

Words to write:

smack	screen	fled
drown	sled	unseen
ballgown	backpack	downtown

Here is how a beginning chart will look:

red	green	brown	black
	queen		

Here is how a completed chart will look:

red	green	brown	black
shed	queen	crown	attack
coed	between	touchdown	knack
fled	unseen	ballgown	smack
sled	screen	drown	backpack
		downtown	

APPLYING STRATEGIES WHEN READING AND WRITING

Many second-grade students are reading and writing well at this time of year. **You may want to look at some March writing samples of your struggling students, comparing them to the January samples.** Is the child using the *Word Wall* and other words displayed in the room to correctly spell most words? Can you read the invented spelling of other words? Is there movement for most children from a letter-by-letter sound-match strategy to a spelling pattern strategy? The word **place** spelled **p-l-a-s-e** shows progression in word knowledge from the letter-by-letter spelling **p-l-a-s.**

You may also want to assess reading level and use of word strategies, particularly for those children whose reading level was still first grade or below in January. Can they now read a more difficult passage—with word accuracy of 90-95% and adequate comprehension—than they could two months ago? When reading at that instructional level, do their errors demonstrate use of context and/or beginning letter-sounds? Are they making some self-corrections? **Remember that all children will not read at the same level, but they should all be developing strategies and showing some growth in the difficulty of the text they can read.** Daily reading and writing will help all children improve. **Look at what your children know to decide what you need to teach. Plan your minilessons for writing and word instruction activities so that most of the children can learn something new and improve their word knowledge. Use individual conference time during writing and self-selected reading to help those who need a nudge and would profit from one-on-one instruction on their own level.**

APRIL

April is here, spring has sprung! Vacation is on everyone's mind, including teachers. We are in the final quarter of the school year and this is probably the most difficult. Some children (and teachers!) have spring fever. The longer days bring soccer and baseball practice in the early evening. Parents are working in the yard at night or car pooling more often. Children are on a busier schedule, so finding time for reading and homework becomes a problem for some. Children have been working hard (like their teachers), and they are looking forward to a spring break. Other children are having such a good time with all their friends and enjoying school activities, that they would rather just stay in school year-round where they are successful and happy! We have known both kinds of students—and both kinds of teachers. We hope that everyone can enjoy a spring break and settle down for the last push. When children see themselves as successful readers and writers, they can and will continue to grow and learn. For these children the literacy journey is a true "ride" and spring won't stop them!

MONTH AT A GLANCE

By the end of April, you will have reviewed the following:

- *Be a Mind Reader* and other strategies for reviewing Word Wall words

- *Guess the Covered Word* with paragraphs and unusually short and long words

- *Making Words* lessons where the children lead the sorts

- *Reading/Writing Rhymes* with ar, art, orn, ear, eer patterns

- *Using Words You Know* (animal names) to decode and spell words

WORD WALL

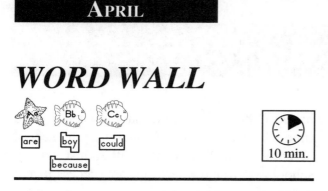

10 min.

April 15th is coming. **Get ready to pay your income taxes and put the last word on the wall! In most classrooms, we try to get the last new words on the wall around mid-April. That gives us six weeks to review these words and greatly increases the chance that children will still be able to read and/or spell these words when they return to school in the fall.** Although *Word Wall* is helpful to your fast learners, who need some daily practice with handwriting and who profit greatly from the *"On-the-Back"* transfer to writing activities, it is not these students who need a *Word Wall* most. **The *Word Wall* is most helpful to children for whom learning the abstract, connecting, "often not spelled the way they sound" words is a huge chore!** Better to put up just over 100 words by mid-April and do lots of practice until the end of the year than to keep adding words. Fast word learners have probably already learned any words you might add and you won't have enough time to practice with your children who struggle to learn them.

Be a Mind Reader

Of all the *Word Wall* activities, this may become the children's favorite. In *Be a Mind Reader*, you can pick one word and give five clues. The children number their papers from 1-5 as always, but this time they are to guess the word you have chosen. Give five clues to the word you have chosen and let students write a guess after each clue is given. If a new clue confirms a student's previous guess, he can write the same word on the line that matches the new clue number. As you progress to the fifth clue, the word that you have in mind should become more obvious. By the last clue everyone should have the word. But who read the teacher's mind and got it on the fourth clue? the third? the second? or maybe even the first clue?

Here are some clues for a *Be a Mind Reader* activity. All the second-grade words listed on page 20 would be on the *Word Wall*. **Give the clues one at a time and allow each student time to make a guess and write it on his paper.**

Be a Mind Reader

1. It is one of the words on the wall.

2. It has five letters in it.

3. It begins with the letter **r**. (Now we are narrowing it down, but which one?)

4. It has only one syllable. (Now we are down to three.)

5. It makes sense in this sentence: Yes, you are _____. (right)

"Now everyone has **right** on the last line, but who was the mind reader? Raise your hand if you had **right** on line four." (Lots of hands.) "Raise your hand if you had **right** on line three." (A few hands.) "Raise your hand if you had **right** on line two." (Usually a hand—if someone is lucky!) "Raise your hand if you had **right** on line 1." (Miraculously, given the odds, every once in a while someone guesses the one word from all the *Word Wall* words that the teacher was thinking of. That is the child who read her mind!)

ON-THE-BACK ACTIVITIES
(RHYMES AND ENDINGS)

5 min.

In addition to *Be a Mind Reader*, **we want to continue practicing how to spell words with endings and also using rhyming formats to help spell lots of words. Once most children get good at this, they can also learn how to do both things at one time.** Here is an easy rhyming format with endings added. **Brown** is a color word being focused on. **The teacher will read a sentence in which the children need to identify a word that rhymes with** *brown*—**and has an ending added**—**and then write it:**

The princess was **crowned** in the play.

Her **gowns** were gold and white.

We went **downtown** to see the circus.

The **clowns** made us laugh.

One was **frowning** and acting silly.

You could also do this with the harder format, using five different words to review and add endings to. Pretend your students have just practiced the words **float, joke, quit, trip,** and **write.** Some sentences the teacher could use to identify rhyming words with endings are:

> Ben will not go on any **trips** during April.
>
> Travis is not **joking**.
>
> Karen is **writing** in a journal.
>
> Kevin is **quitting** the baseball team.
>
> Sam got hurt when he **floated** into the wall of the pool.

When children are writing, they often need to spell a word that rhymes with one of the *Word Wall* **words and has an ending added. Make sure, however, that everyone spells the word aloud correctly before writing it because this could be frustrating for many of your children.**

ON-THE-BACK ACTIVITY
(FIVE DIFFERENT WORDS THAT RHYME WITH WORD WALL WORDS)

5 min.

There is another rhyming *"On-the-Back"* format which we have introduced before which is worth mentioning again this month. It is harder but closer to what children actually have to do to use the *Word Wall* words to spell a word they need while writing. **To do this rhyming format, make sure that all the words you call out for them to write on the front have some words that rhyme and share the same spelling pattern.** You might call out the words: **make, thing, mail, went,** and **will**. Help the children to notice that all these words are helpful words (perhaps starred or stickered words on your wall). Tell them that you are going to pretend to be writing and you need to spell a word that rhymes with one of these five words. Tell them some sentences you might be writing, emphasizing the word you need to spell. Let them decide which of the five helpful words they wrote on the front will help you.

Betty put new **string** on her kite.

Mark ran fast and I took a **spill.**

Laura **spent** her money at the ballgame.

The **trail** in the park was long.

Ben got new **brakes** on my bike.

GUESS THE COVERED WORD

Guess the covered word.

20 min.

Once you have begun to use this new rhyming format, alternate it with the easier one in which your sentences use rhymes for only one of the words. The harder format helps children who are ready to think of a rhyming word that can help them spell lots of words. The easier format is most important for children who are still developing their sense of rhyme and how rhyme helps us spell.

Guess the Covered Word lessons provide practice with cross-checking by demonstrating to students that guesses based solely on meaning or beginning letters or length are not good guesses. But **when you combine all three and come up with a word that makes sense, has all the beginning letters up to the vowel, and is about the right length, you can make a very good guess at an unknown word.** Remember to have students make two or three guesses for each word with no letters showing; then uncover all the letters up to the vowel. If possible, include some unusually short and long key words in the words you cover so that they become sensitive to word length. Here is an example related to April that has some unusually short and long words.

April

In April we can have fun at the **playground.** **Youngsters** swing and slide. Donna plays on the **bars.** Matt **runs** on the grass. Travis plays **basketball** with his friends. Our **classmates** come to watch us. They **yell** when we play well. What do you **do** in April?

MAKING WORDS

20 min.

The lessons that are the most meaningful are connected to what the students are studying. You will notice that the children who like *Making Words* will begin to guess the mystery word the minute they see the letters. We want to continue lessons connected to the stories you are reading and the themes or units you are studying. You may want to continue to focus children's attention on the blends. Lots of practice will help the struggling readers to see these beginning letters as clusters and not to look at just the first letter but all the letters up to the vowel. Remember that when we sort the words, we first sort for the beginning letters, then for endings (if there are any), and finally for rhymes. We want to end up with the rhyming words lined up one under another so that we can use them to read and spell a few new words. Also, remember that we want the children to find the patterns. Early in the year, we would get the children to sort by saying:

> "Who can go up and find the two words that begin with **ch**?"
>
> "Who can go up and find the words with the **ing** endings?"
>
> "Who can go up and find all the words with the **each** spelling pattern?"

By now we would say:

> "Who can go up and sort the words into words with the same beginning letters?"
>
> "Who can go up and find some words with the same endings?"
>
> "Who can go up and sort the words into rhymes with the same spelling pattern?"

Children need to look at words and see patterns. By this time in the year, our questions should be leading them to that kind of independent thinking about the words they see.

Sometimes the teacher lets the children decide what to sort for—they like this! They lead the class just as their teacher has all year. If they do not choose a sort that you want to emphasize, then you can add it at the end. Here are some April lessons for your class.

Secret Word: detective
Letters: e, e, e, i, c, d, t, t, v
Make: it, tie, die, ice, dice, diet/tide/tied/edit, detect, device, deceive, detective
Sort: words with **de** as the first chunk, -ie, -ice
Transfer: pie, spice, twice, price

Secret Word: project
Letters: e, o, j, t, p, r, c
Make: to, top/pot, pet, jet, jot, rot, cot, crop, core, tore, rope, port, poet, crept, project
Sort: cr-, -et, -ot, -op, -ore
Transfer: met, slot, flop, score

Secret Word: playing
Letters: a, i, g, l, p, n, y
Make: in, an, pan, pin, pig, pay, play, plan, pain, gain, plain, paying, playing
Sort: pl-, -ing (ending), -an, -in, -ay, -ain
Transfer: scan, skin, spray, spraying

Secret Word: glasses
Letters: a, e, g, l, s, s, s
Make: as, gas/sag, lag, sea, seas, seal/sale, legs, lass, glass, seals/sales, lasses, glasses
Sort: gl-, plurals (**s** and **es**), -ag, -ass
Tranfser: brag, drag, class, classes

Secret Word: crickets
Letters: e, i, c, c, k, r, t, s
Make: it, kit, sit, tie, irk, ice, rice, tire/tier, kite, tick, trick, tricks, cricket, crickets
Sort: plurals, -it, -ice, -ick
Transfer: split, twice, spice, clicks

Secret Word: carton
Letters: a, o, o, c, n, r, t
Make: to, at, cat, car, can, tan, tar/rat/art, cart, coat, torn, corn, acorn, actor, carton, cartoon
Sort: -at, -an, -art, -orn
Transfer: chat, scan, thorn, scorn

Secret Word: waitress
Letters: a, e, i, r, s, s, t, w
Make: at, sat, saw/was, war, wart, east, west, wire, tire, wait, waits/waist, waste, water, wrist, write, waste, waiter, waitress
Sort: wr-, waist-waste (homophones), -at, -ire
Transfer: splat, scat, fire, inspire

Secret Word: savings
Letters: a, i, g, n, s, s, v
Make: an, in, sin, sag/gas, nag, van, vans, vain, gain, sang, snag, sign/sing, assign, savings
Sort: plurals, -an, -ag, -ain
Transfer: bran, shag, strain, brains

READING/ WRITING RHYMES

READING & WRITING

sand	mice
stand	twice
hand	nice

RHYMES

20 min.

The steps to a *Reading/Writing Rhymes* lesson are:

1. Distribute the onset deck to the students. If initial sounds still need practice, have them say each onset as you pass them out.

2. Once all the onset cards are distributed, write the spelling pattern you are working 10-12 times on a piece of chart paper.

3. Invite the children who have a card that they think makes a word to come up and place their card next to one of the written spelling patterns and pronounce the word. If the word is indeed a real word, use the word in a sentence and write it on a chart. If the word is not a real word, explain why you cannot write it on the chart. If a word is a real word and does rhyme but has a different spelling pattern, such as **planned** with **and**, explain that it rhymes but has a different pattern; include it on the bottom of the chart with an asterisk next to it. Write people's names with capitals and, if a word can be a name and not a name, such as **Bill** and **bill**, write it both ways.

4. When all the children who think they can spell words with their beginning letters and the spelling pattern have come up, call children up to make the words not yet there by saying something like:

"I think the person with the **tw** card could come up here and add **tw** to **ine** to make a word we know."

If you use all the patterns you wrote to begin the chart, add as many more as needed.

5. If you can think of some good, longer words that rhyme and have that spelling pattern, add them to the list. Spell and write the longer words since children do not have the extra letters needed to spell them.

6. Once the chart of rhyming words is written, work together in a shared writing format to write a couple of sentences using lots of rhyming words.

7. Give the students a few minutes to work individually or with friends to write some silly text using as many rhyming words as they can.

For this month we have chosen the spelling patterns **ar, art, orn** and **ear/eer**. The eer and ear patterns are done on the same chart. Here are some words you can make with these patterns, along with the words that rhyme but do not have the same spelling pattern (*). (You may want to temporarily "lose" the **f** card when doing the **art** pattern!)

"-ar" words

bar, car, azar, far, jar, mar, par, scar, spar, star, tar, ajar, cigar, boxcar, *are

---

"-art" words

art, cart, chart, dart, mart, part, smart, start, tart, apart, depart, restart, *heart

---

"-orn" words

born, corn, horn, morn, scorn, sworn, thorn, torn, worn, acorn, *mourn

---

"-ear" / "-eer" words

clear, dear, ear, fear, gear, hear, near, rear, smear, spear, tear, year, appear

cheer, deer, jeer, peer, sheer, steer, veer, career

USING WORDS YOU KNOW

20 min.

Using Words You Know **is an activity that helps students see that you can use what you know to figure out something they do not know.** For example, second grade students know the animal names: **dog, cat, pig,** and **hen.**

1. Display these animal words on the board or a chart, and talk about the words.

2. Identify the spelling patterns (**og, at, ig,** and **en**).

3. Have the students make 4 columns on their paper. Head these with the names of the animals and underline the spelling patterns.

4. Show them some one-syllable words written on index cards. Have them write these words under the word with the same pattern, using the rhyme to pronounce the words. End with a word with two syllables, so the children can see how to chunk words and use this knowledge for bigger words.

5. Say some one-syllable words and have the children decide how to spell them by deciding which word they rhyme with. Then, say some two-syllable words; see if they can write them using the spelling pattern in the last syllable, and familiar words or word parts (prefixes) to help them decide on the spelling.

Words you know:

d<u>og</u>   c<u>at</u>   p<u>ig</u>   h<u>en</u>

Words to read:

sat	fog	fig
hog	pen	when
jog	gnat	flat
then	clog	chat
twig	smog	pigpen
nonfat	bullfrog	unclog

Words to write:

bog	brat	wig	big
den	splat	bulldog	chitchat
combat	shindig	amen	unpen

The finished chart will look like:

d<u>og</u>	c<u>at</u>	p<u>ig</u>	h<u>en</u>
fog	sat	fig	pen
hog	gnat	twig	when
jog	flat	pigpen	then
clog	chat		pigpen
smog	nonfat		
bullfrog			
unclog			
bog	brat	wig	den
bulldog	splat	big	amen
	chitchat	shindig	unpen
	combat		

APPLYING STRATEGIES WHEN READING AND WRITING

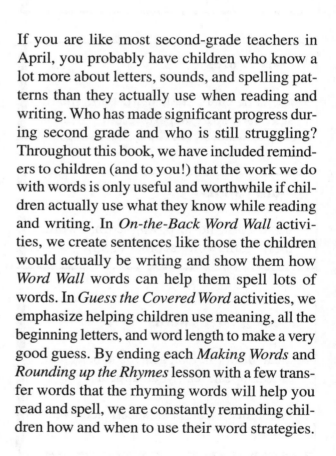

If you are like most second-grade teachers in April, you probably have children who know a lot more about letters, sounds, and spelling patterns than they actually use when reading and writing. Who has made significant progress during second grade and who is still struggling? Throughout this book, we have included reminders to children (and to you!) that the work we do with words is only useful and worthwhile if children actually use what they know while reading and writing. In *On-the-Back Word Wall* activities, we create sentences like those the children would actually be writing and show them how *Word Wall* words can help them spell lots of words. In *Guess the Covered Word* activities, we emphasize helping children use meaning, all the beginning letters, and word length to make a very good guess. By ending each *Making Words* and *Rounding up the Rhymes* lesson with a few transfer words that the rhyming words will help you read and spell, we are constantly reminding children how and when to use their word strategies.

In spite of all this concerted effort, there are some children who "just don't get it!" They participate and seem to understand our word activities but when they read and write, they don't transfer what they know! There are two ways to help children use more of what they know.

The first opportunity occurs during writing conferences when we are helping children to fix their spelling on a piece they are going to publish. In first grade, much of what children write stays in first draft form and their invented spellings are applauded. In second grade, we want to focus on editing their own work—looking back to see if they spelled words correctly even during the first draft. We want to encourage a spelling consciousness by having them ask themselves when rereading, "Does it look right?" When we publish a book or prepare pieces for display on the bulletin board, we do help the children to spell the words correctly so that other people can read what they wrote. There are many words which children use in their writing which they can't be expected to know how to spell. When we are conferencing with them, we simply acknowledge the good efforts shown in their invented spellings and then write the correct spelling above it. But at other times, we use the writing conference as the teachable moment to nudge them forward in their use of spelling patterns. Imagine that you are editing with a child at this time of the year and the child has written the word **played** as playd. Ask that child:

> "What is the ending of that word? When we write *Word Wall* words with endings, what letters do we add to words? Yes, that is right. We add "ed." Now check your ending and correct this word."

Writing conferences are a great opportunity to individualize what we teach children. For some children, we just praise the invented spelling efforts and fix the spelling. For other children we use the opportunity to point out things about letters, sounds, and spelling patterns that they know when doing words but are not applying as they are writing.

To coach children to use what they know while reading, we do some short (10-12 minutes) individual or very small group coaching sessions in which we lead them through the steps at the exact moment they need to use them. We use text that they haven't read before and which is going to contain some words they need to figure out. Having text at instructional level (5-10 errors per 100 words) is ideal. Explain to the children that the book will have words they haven't learned yet and that the purpose of these lessons is to see how good readers figure out words they don't know. Good readers are usually reading books they can read easily and fluently, stopping only once in a while to decode a word. Have a child begin reading, and when the child comes to a word and stops, say:

> **"Put your finger on the word and say all the letters."**

Good readers look at all the letters in each word. Children who are struggling with reading tend to look quickly at the word, and, if they don't instantly recognize it, they stop and wait for someone to tell them the word. Asking them to say all the letters forces them to look at all the letters. **Sometimes, after saying all the letters, they correctly pronounce the word!** This is proof that they aren't in the habit of looking at all the letters and you should let them know what they have done by saying something like:

> "That's right. There are lots of words we see when we are reading that we don't recognize right away, but when we look at all the letters, we can sometimes figure them out. Good job! Continue reading."

If, after saying the letter, the child does not say the word, you should say:

> **"Keep your finger on that word and finish the sentence."**

It may seem foolish to have the child keep his or her finger there, but young children's print tracking skills are not nearly as good as ours. Many children can't use the context of the sentence and the letters in the unknown word to figure out a word because once they get to the end of the sentence, they can't quickly look back and find the troublesome word. **Keeping one finger on the word allows the child to quickly track back.** If, after finishing the sentence, the child correctly pronounces the word, say something like:

> "Right. You can figure out lots of words you don't know if you use your finger to keep track of where the word is, finish the sentence, and then do like we do in *Guess the Covered Word*— guess a word that makes sense, begins with all the right letters, and is the right length. Continue reading."

If the child still does not get the word, you have three possible cues to point out. **If there is a good picture clue (which the child has ignored!), you could say,**

> "What animal do you see in the picture that begins with l?"

If the troublesome word can be decoded based on one of the patterns on the *World Wall* or used frequently during other word activities, you could say,

> "Let's see. The word is spelled **t-r-a-s-h.** We know that **c-r-a-s-h** spells **crash.** Can you make this word rhyme with **crash**?

If there is nothing in the picture to help and the word is not easily decodable based on a familiar rhyming word, you can give an explicit context clue. Imagine that the word is **ridiculous** in the sentence:

> That is a **ridiculous** hat.

We say to the child:

> "Well, let's see. **Do you think it says, 'That is a ripe hat' or 'that is a ridiculous hat'?**

We make our alternative word begin with the correct letters but be so unmeaningful that the child will make the right choice. We then say:

"Good. That was a hard word but you got it! Let's continue reading."

Explaining this in writing makes it sound much longer and more complicated than it actually is. When we are coaching a child to learn to use what he or she knows (but isn't using), we choose text in which the child is going to come to an unknown word every second or third sentence. When the child stops at a word, we go through the following steps:

1. Put your finger on the word and say all the letters.

2. Keep your finger there and finish the sentence.

3. What do you see in the picture that starts with—?

   Or, we see that the word is spelled—. We can spell—. Can you make this rhyme with—?

4. Finally, if all above cueing fails:

   "Let's see. Do you think it says, 'That is a ridiculous hat or that is a ripe hat?'"

When the child gets the word after any of our cueing, we congratulate the child and point out which strategy the child used that helped him or her figure out the word.

If a child miscalls a word (instead of the usual struggling reader strategy of stopping on the word and waiting to be told), we wait for the child to finish the sentence, repeat the sentence as the child read it, and point out that it didn't make sense. Then we take the child through as many steps as necessary.

Most children do not need the kind of one-on-one or very small group coaching described here; but for those who do, short coaching sessions held a few times each week, even at this time of year, make a world of difference in their ability to use what they know when they need to use it!

MAY/JUNE

The last month of the school year is finally here—even for year-round students. All children and their teachers look forward to a break from the school routine. This is the time to continue sharing some good books and good authors and to encourage reading as recreation. It is for many of us! What better recreation on a hot day than to get lost in a good book under a shady tree. It is a busy time with thoughts of baseball, swimming, the pool, the beach, vacations, camp, fireworks, and Fourth of July ahead of us—all those "summertime things." Just a few more weeks and these children will leave second grade. Many will be expected to have learned all about words and reading. They will now be expected to read to learn. Are they ready? If you have been working all year this is a wonderful time to reap your rewards. We marvel at second-grade students who are reading and writing far beyond their years. We celebrate the gains made by our struggling readers; some have come so far this year. We realize that it is not where they are that matters, but how far they have come. Often growth in reading and writing is not steady, but comes in spurts. When we see these spurts—and for some it happens in second grade—it is rewarding to both the teacher and the child. Both have been working hard! **During our last month, we will try to consolidate what we have been teaching and what they have learned this year.**

MONTH AT A GLANCE

By the end of the school year (May/June), you will have reviewed the following:

- *Word Wall* words and the many words you can write with rhyming words and endings

- *On-the-Back* activities to consolidate the word learning with words on the wall

- *Guess the Covered Word* with paragraphs and two and three-letter clusters at the beginning of the covered words

- *Making Word*s with the letters y and z and some summer words

- *Reading/Writing Rhymes* with the spelling patterns **oy, ow,** and then using several charts to write some rhymes

- *Using Words You Know* (number words) to read and write lots of other words

- Consolidating many strategies taught and assessing the progress your students have made in their word learning

WORD WALL

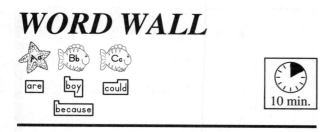

⏱ 10 min.

This is the month to try to consolidate the spelling of the words on the wall, spelling words with endings, and seeing how some words help you spell lots of other words. Continue working with the important **s**, **ed**, and **ing** endings and perhaps show them how they can spell **jumpy**, **rainy**, and **buggy** by adding **y** to **jump**, **rain** and **bug**; and **nicely**, **friendly** by adding **ly** to **nice** and **friend**. You can add **er** and **est** to **new**, **little** and **pretty**. **Tell, jump, kick, truck**, and **teach** can become the person who does them by adding **er**. Continue working with both rhyming formats and hope that all your children will leave second grade with a firm concept that words that rhyme usually have the same spelling pattern and that many of your children will be spelling lots of words based on other rhyming words they can spell.

You now have a good number of words on your wall that have opposites and children enjoy *Word Wall* **"riddles" when you call out the words by giving an opposite clue.**

Word Wall Riddles

1. Word number one begins with the letter **p** and is the opposite of **ugly**.

2. Word number two begins with the letter **g** and is the opposite of **boy**.

3. Word number three begins with the letter **d** and is the opposite of **do**.

4. Word number four begins with the letters **qu** and is the opposite of **start**.

5. Word number five begins with the letter **r** and is the opposite of **wrong**.

1) pretty 2) girl 3) don't 4) quit 5) right

Perhaps the favorite *Word Wall* review activity of the children is *Be a Mind Reader*. In *Be a Mind Reader*, you pick one word and you give five clues. The children number their papers from 1-5 as always, but they know they are trying to guess the word you are thinking of. As the clues continue, the word which the teacher has in mind becomes more obvious. By the last clue everyone should have the word. But who read the teacher's mind and got it on the fourth clue? The third? The second? Or maybe even the first clue? Here are some clues for a *Be a Mind Reader*. All the words listed for second grade (page 20) are on the wall. Here are the clues. Can you get it before the last clue is given?

How to Do *Be a Mind Reader*

1. It is one of the words on the wall. (This is always the first clue—much to the consternation of the children!)

2. It has four letters. (This eliminates a whole lot of words—but there are still a lot of possible words.)

3. It begins with the letter **w**. (Now, we're narrowing it down but which one?)

4. It ends with a "t." (Well, it's either **went**, **what** or **won't**, but which one?)

5. It makes sense in the sentence: "I _____ to the store."

   Now everyone has **went** on the last line, but who read my mind? Raise your hand if you had **went** on line 4 (Lots of hands.)

Line 3 (A few hands.)

Line 2 (Usually a hand.)

Line 1 (Miraculously, given the odds, every once in a while someone guesses the one word from all the *Word Wall* words that the teacher was thinking of. They really must be mind readers!)

(**Answer:** went)

---

1. It is one of the words on the *Word Wall*.

2. It has five letters.

3. It begins with the vowel "a" (about, after, again).

4. It ends with **out**.

5. It makes sense in this sentence: The story is _____ a fish swimming.

(**Answer:** about)

---

1. It is one of the words on the *Word Wall*.

2. It has more than 3 letters.

3. It is a compound word (outside, into, sometimes).

4. The word begins with a vowel.

5. It make sense in this sentence: The boy went _____ the water.

(**Answer:** into)

---

1. It is one of the words on the *Word Wall*.

2. It has 5 letters.

3. It is a homonym (write/right, there/their/they're).

4. It begins with **th**.

5. It makes sense in this sentence: Put the shells over _____.

(**Answer:** there)

GUESS THE COVERED WORD

Guess the covered word.

20 min.

It is time to consolidate the strategies of looking at all the letters up to the vowel, looking at how long the word is, and thinking what would make sense in order to decode unknown words. **Try to get the children to verbalize the strategy.** Ideally, they should all know that:

> **"When you see a word you don't know, you can usually figure it out if you say "blank" and finish the sentence and then go back and guess a word that has all the right beginning letters and makes sense in the sentence. It is good to look at how long the word is too."**

Perhaps you would like to write some paragraphs such as the following and cover the underlined words with two self-adhesive notes. Read the paragraph, one sentence at a time, and make guesses for the covered word. As children continue reading, they should be using the whole context of what they have read so far to figure out the covered words. Be sure to have your self-adhesive notes cut to size so that word length is obvious. When you remove the first self-adhesive note, show them all the letters up to the vowel.

You don't always have to use the names of your children in *Guess the Covered Word* activities, as you have seen. Using the names of your students often keeps them actively involved, trying to figure out what happened to whom. You can also use this activity when you want to write some sentences that connect to your theme/unit. Remember to move some of the words to be guessed to various positions in the sentence. Be sure children read the whole sentence, skipping over the covered word, before they give their guesses. **Here is a May paragraph that uses big words and two and three-letter clusters at the beginning of the words. Notice that the words are placed in a variety of positions.**

May

We plant flowers in our garden. We plant bright flowers to look at all summer. We also plant vegetables in a garden. My favorites are tomatoes and peppers. We water our garden to keep it growing. Harvesting the vegetables is the best part. Do you have a garden?

MAKING WORDS

making words

20 min.

There are so many possibilities for *Making Words* lessons as the year draws to a close. We are reviewing many of the patterns and letter sounds we have had all year, and, for many, they are becoming automatic. **We have included some lessons that use the letters *y* and *z*.** It just seems a shame to have made those letters and not used them even once! Do them in any order you choose and watch to see how long it takes before the kids figure out the mystery word! Be sure to **review that important names, like people names and names of days of the week, begin with capital letters.** The days of the week make excellent lessons at any grade level. **Many teachers like to have the letter *y* card be a different color from all the rest of the letters. It can't be the same color as the consonants or the vowels because sometimes it is a consonant and sometimes it is a vowel! In addition to the usual things to sort for, lessons containing *y* words are sorted for the three sounds of *y* as in *yam*, *fly*, and *family*.**

Secret Word: family
Letters: a, i, f, l, m, y
Make: if, my, may/yam, Fay, fly, aim, ail, fail, mail, film, filmy, family
Sort: y(i)-, y(e)-, -ay, -aim, -ail
Transfer: stray, claim, jail, snail

Secret Word: cooking
Letters: i, o, o, c, g, k, n
Make: in, ink/kin, coo, coon, cook, nook, nick, coin, oink, cooing, cooking
Sort: ing (ending), -in, -ook
Transfer: spin, spinning, brook, shook

Secret Word: pretzels
Letters: e, e, l, p, r, s, t, z
Make: pet, set, see, tree, step/pest, zest, rest, re-set, trees, steep, sleep, sleet, preset, pester, pretzels
Sort: sl-, st-, s (plural), -et, ee, -est, -eep
Transfer: glee, chest, sweep, chests

Secret Word: diamond
Letters: a, i, o, d, d, m, n
Make: an, Dan, dad, did, add, aid, aim, mad, man, main, maid, mind, moan, nomad, diamond
Sort: -an, -ad, -aid
Transfer: scan, glad, grad, paid

Secret Word: parents
Letters: a, e, n, p, r, s, t
Make: at, ant, art/rat, pat, pet, set, sent, rent, rant, pant, past, paste, pants, parents
Sort: s(plural), -ant, -at, -ent, -et
Transfer: plant, slant, spent, events

Secret Word: scallops

Letters: a, o, c, l, l, p, s, s

Make: all, sap, cap, lap/pal, call, clap, slap, soap, pass, class, clasp/claps, scalp, scalps, scallops

Sort: s(plural), -ap, -ass, -all

Transfer: stalls, trap, flaps

Secret Word: summertime

Letters: e, e, i, u, m, m, m, r, s, t

Make: see, set, sir, sit, meet, must, rust, mist, stem, stir, tree, miser, steer/trees, summer, summertime

Sort: -ir, -ee, -ust

Transfer: fir, crust, trust, free

Secret Word: seashells

Letters: a, e, e, h, l, l, s, s, s

Make: he, she, see, sea, sell, seal/sale, heal, shell, leash, easel, easels, shells, leashes, seashells

Sort: s and es (plurals), -ell, -eal

Transfer: spell, jell, squeal, squeals

READING/WRITING RHYMES

If your second-grade students are like most, they will enjoy *Reading/Writing Rhymes* up to and including the last day of school. They are fun for the children to do in pairs or small groups. They keep children actively thinking and learning about words. *Reading/Writing Rhymes* also helps second-grade students learn the different vowel patterns that will make them better readers and writers in the years to come.

The steps to a *Reading/Writing Rhymes* lesson are:

1. Distribute the onset deck to the students. If initial sounds still need practice, have them say each onset as you pass them out.

2. Once all the onset cards are distributed, write the spelling pattern you are working with 10-12 times on a piece of chart paper.

3. Invite the children who have a card that they think makes a word to come up and place their card next to one of the written spelling patterns and pronounce the word. If the word is indeed a real word, use the word in a sentence and write it on a chart. If the word is not a real word, explain why you cannot write it on the chart. If a word is a real word and does rhyme but has a different spelling pattern, such as **trail** with **whale**, explain that it rhymes but has a different pattern, and include it on the

bottom of the chart with an asterisk next to it. Write people's names with capitals, and, if a word can be a name and not a name, such as **Jack** and **jack**, write it both ways.

4. When all the children who think they can spell words with their beginning letters and the spelling pattern have come up, call children up to make the words not yet there by saying something like:

"I think the person with the **br** card could come up here and add **br** to **ake** to make a word we know."

If you use all the patterns you wrote to begin the chart, add as many more as needed.

5. If you can think of some good, longer words that rhyme and have that spelling pattern, add them to the list. Spell and write the longer words since children do not have the extra letters needed to spell them.

6. Once the chart of rhyming words is written, work together in a shared writing format to write a couple of sentences using lots of rhyming words.

7. Give the students a few minutes to work individually or with friends to write some silly text using as many rhyming words as they can.

For this month we have chosen the spelling patterns **oy**, and **y(i)** and will let the children write rhymes from two or more charts we have already made. Here are some words you can make with these patterns, along with the words that rhyme but do not have the same spelling pattern (*).

"-oy" words

boy, coy, joy, ploy, Roy, soy, toy, Troy, annoy, enjoy

"-y" words

by, cry, dry, fly, fry, try, my, pry, shy, sky, sly, spry, spy, sty, why, *tie, *hi, *buy, *eye, *guy, *high, *thigh

---

To do a lesson with many rhymes you are reviewing, pull out your charts from months past. Let's use some rhyming words we did in December.

-ill	-op	-ot	-ug	-ut
bill	bop	blot	bug	but
dill	chop	cot	chug	cut
chill	cop	clot	drug	gut
drill	crop	dot	hug	hut
fill	drop	got	jug	nut
grill	flop	knot	lug	rut
hill	hop	lot	mug	shut
ill	mop	not	plug	smut
Jill	plop	plot	pug	strut
kill	pop	pot	rug	*what
mill	prop	rot	shrug	*mutt
pill	shop	shot	slug	*putt
sill	stop	slot	smug	
skill	top	spot	snug	
still	*swap	tot	thug	
thrill		trot	tug	
will		*squat	*ugh	
Will		*yacht		
anthill				
fullfill				
uphill				

Here is a rhyme you can read with your class. Second-grade students are so good at doing this—better than most teachers!

> **Bill** and **Jill** had a **spill** going **uphill**. They saw a **bug** in their **jug** and gave a **shrug**. They could not **stop**. They had to **shop**. Off they went with a **hop**. They bought a **pot** and a **cot**, a **drill** and a **grill**. What a **thrill** for **Bill** and **Jill**!

USING WORDS YOU KNOW

20 min.

Using *Words You Know* is an activity that helps students see that you can use what you know to figure out something you do not know. For example, second-grade students know the number names: **three, five, nine,** and **ten**.

1. Display these number words on the board or a chart, and talk about the words.

2. Identify the spelling patterns (**ee, ive, ine, and en**)

3. Have the students make 4 columns on their paper. Head these with the names of the numbers and underline the spelling patterns.

4. Show them some one-syllable words written on index cards. Have them write these words under the word with the same pattern, using the rhyme to pronounce the words. End with a word with two syllables, so the children can see how to chunk words and use this knowledge for bigger words.

5. Say some one-syllable words and have the children decide how to spell them by deciding which word they rhyme with. Then, say some two-syllable words: see if they can write them using the spelling pattern in the last syllable, along with familiar words or word parts (prefixes), to help them decide on the spelling.

128

APPLYING STRATEGIES WHEN READING AND WRITING

Words you know:

thr<u>ee</u>   f<u>i</u>v<u>e</u>   n<u>i</u>n<u>e</u>   t<u>e</u>n

Words to read:

bee	den	jive
mine	free	when
knee	dive	drive
then	amen	strive
pigpen	whine	airline
arrive	peewee	beehive

Words to write:

men	pine	hive
live	flee	glee
twine	agree	playpen
spine	baseline	alive

This is how the finished chart will look:

thr<u>ee</u>	f<u>i</u>v<u>e</u>	n<u>i</u>n<u>e</u>	t<u>e</u>n
bee	jive	mine	den
free	dive	whine	when
knee	drive	airline	then
peewee	strive		amen
beehive	arrive		pigpen
	beehive		
flee	hive	pine	men
glee	live	twine	playpen
agree	alive	spine	
		baseline	

Don't give up! During editing conferences, remind them that every word needs a vowel in it and help them to find and use the correct vowel patterns when writing words. Keep working with individuals or very small groups for short coaching sessions in which you remind them to use what they know when they need to use it. Your children may not all be perfect at doing this, but by the time school is out, they should all know that when you come to a word you don't know, you can:

1. Put your finger on the word and say all the letters.

2. Keep your finger there and finish the sentence.

3. Look for something in the picture that starts with these letters.

   or

   Look at how the word is spelled to see if you know another word with that spelling pattern.

   or

   Make it make sense and begin with the right letters.

ASSESSING THEIR PROGRESS

Assessing at the end of the year means looking at how far they have come. Most teachers repeat whatever assessments they did halfway through the year. Many schools have assessment teams that go to each class and administer Informal Reading Inventories to all children to determine their instructional reading levels. Information that will be helpful to next year's teacher is compiled in some kind of growth portfolio. In many schools, there are some items (focused writing samples, IRI results, developmental spelling tests, etc.) which are included in all portfolios. Individual teachers—and sometimes children—then choose a few additional pieces to represent their growth. A short write-up by the teacher is usually included for each child. This short narrative describes the child's literacy early in the year and the growth each child has made. Children come to us at all different stages of literacy development. Some children develop literacy, including decoding and spelling strategies, quickly and seemingly effortlessly. Other children take longer and need lots of practice, nudging, and coaching. Our assessment techniques should focus on progress and document growth. Such assessment allows to us do the kind of multilevel instruction all classrooms of children need and allows us to celebrate how far each child has come instead of bemoaning the fact that they are not all "on grade level."

OVERVIEW: A BALANCED LITERACY PROGRAM FOR SECOND GRADE

This chapter provides an overview of the balanced literacy program of which the phonics and spelling activities described in this book are one component.

Each year, six million children begin school in our public schools. Many of these children can be immediately identified as "at-risk"—the currently popular descriptor for those children who will not learn to read and write well enough to achieve a basic level of literacy and a high school diploma. The number of children at risk varies from community to community and state to state. Nationwide, NAEP results suggest that more than one-third of all nine-year-olds cannot read at the "basic" level. For African-Americans, 61% fail to achieve this basic level (Mullis & Jenkins, 1990).

These statistics have held fairly constant despite decades of expensive attempts to "fix" the problem. Federal fix-ups have generally included a variety of pull-out remediation programs which have spawned huge bureaucracies and have not succeeded in eliminating the risk for very many children. State and local fix-ups often consisted of passing regulations that prohibited children being promoted unless they obtained certain test scores, resulting in huge numbers of retained children. Shepard and Smith (1990) reviewed decades of research on retention. Their data show that retained children perform more poorly when they go to the next grade than they would if they had been promoted without repeating a grade and that almost any alternative is more effective than retention. Their data also suggest that "transition" classes, when they result in children spending another year in the primary grades, have the same ill effects as retention. Dismal as this research is, there is once again a return to these policies in our schools.

Within individual schools or classrooms, in addition to federally provided remediation and state or locally mandated retention, teachers usually try to meet the needs of at-risk children by putting them in a "bottom" reading group and pacing their instruction more slowly. The data on bottom groups does not hold out much hope that this solution will ultimately solve the problem. Children who are placed in the bottom group in first grade generally remain there throughout their elementary school career and almost never learn to read and write up to grade-level standards (Allington, 1983; Allington, 1991).

Against this backdrop, we have the peculiarly American phenomenon of the "pendulum swing." Various approaches to reading come in and out of fashion. In 1990, when we began this endeavor, literature-based reading instruction (commonly referred to as "whole language") was the recommended approach. In 1998, this approach is losing favor and school boards are mandating phonics approaches and purchasing spelling books. The search for the "best way to teach reading" denies the reality of individual differences. Children do not all learn in the same way, and, consequently, approaches with particular emphases are apt to result in some children learning to read and others not. When the pendulum swings to another approach, we may pick up some of those who weren't faring too well under the previous emphasis but lose some who were. Thirty years ago, the first-grade studies which were carried out to determine the best approach concluded that the teacher was more important than the method but that, in general, combination approaches worked better than any single approach (Bond & Dykstra, 1967).

We developed the Four-Blocks Framework to meet two goals. The first goal was to avoid the pendulum-swing and not be trendy but rather to find a way to combine the major approaches to reading instruction. The second goal was to meet the needs of children with a wide range of entering literacy levels without putting them in ability groups.

This project began in the fall of 1989 in one first-grade classroom (Cunningham, Hall & Defee, 1991; Hall, Prevatte & Cunningham, 1995, Cunningham, Hall, & Defee, 1998) This classroom was one of four first-grade classrooms in a large suburban school to which children from the inner city were bussed. The class contained 26 children, half boys and girls, 26 percent African-American. The teacher was an experienced teacher who agreed to work with us to see if we could come up with a "do-able" classroom framework for meeting the dual goals of (1.) providing nonability grouped instruction that met the needs of children with a wide range of entering literacy levels, and (2.) providing children with daily instruction incorporating several reading approaches. During this first year, we developed the instructional framework and assessment procedures. At the end of this year, our success propelled us to involve other first-grade teachers at three schools. We refined the framework to accommodate the teaching styles of 16 unique first-grade teachers.

In the third year, we continued to work with first-grade teachers and children and expanded the program to second grade. From the fourth year on, we have worked with numerous school districts throughout the country to implement this balanced framework in hundreds of first and second grades.

THE INSTRUCTIONAL FRAMEWORK

The instructional framework is the heart of our program. The basic notions of this framework are quite simple, but its implementation is complex. There is a lot of variation depending on how early or late in the year it is and whether the framework is being carried out in first or second grade. There is also much variation attributed to the individual teaching styles of the teacher and the particular makeup of the class being taught. In this section, we will describe the instruction and provide some sense of the variety that allows its implementation in a wide range of classrooms.

In order to meet the goal of providing children with a variety of avenues to becoming literate, instructional time is divided fairly evenly between the four major historical approaches to reading instruction. The 2¼ - 2½ hours allotted to Language Arts is divided among four blocks—Guided Reading, Self-Selected Reading, Writing, and Working with Words—each of which gets 30-40 minutes.

To meet our second goal of providing for a wide range of literacy levels without ability grouping the children, we make the instruction within each block as multilevel as possible. For each block, we will briefly describe some of the formats, materials, cooperative arrangements, etc., we use to achieve this goal of multilevel instruction.

GUIDED READING

In our first several years, we called this the Basal Block because this was the time when the basal reader drove our instruction. In recent years, teachers have branched out to use other materials in addition to or instead of the adopted basal reader. Depending on the time of year, the needs of the class and the personality of the teacher, **Guided Reading lessons are carried out with the system-wide adopted basal, basal readers from previously adopted series, multiple copies of trade books, or multiple copies of books from a variety of publishers, articles from *My Weekly Reader*, or similar magazines and big books, and combinations of these. The purposes of this block are to expose children to a wide range of literature, teach comprehension, and teach children how to read in materials that become increasingly harder. The block usually begins with a discussion led by the teacher to build or review any background knowledge necessary to read the selection. Comprehension strategies are also taught and practiced during this block. The reading is done in a variety of small groups, partners, and individual formats.** Some teachers have a three-ring circus or "Book Clubs" going on (Cunningham, Hall, & Sigmon, 1998). **After the reading is completed, the whole class is called together to discuss the selection and practice strategies. This block sometimes includes writing in response to reading.**

Early in second grade, most of our Guided Reading time is spent in grade-level books or the shared reading of predictable (easier) big books. Comprehension activities often include "doing the book" in which children are given roles and become the characters as the rest of the children read the book. Little books based on the big books are read and reread with partners, then individually or in small groups. Class books and take-home books patterned on the big book are often constructed in shared writing activities. Often the big books read during Guided Reading are chosen because they fit a theme or unit the class is studying, and Guided Reading time floats seamlessly into other unit-oriented activities. Follow-up activities for the book and the theme often occupy some of the afternoon time.

Shared reading of big books continues to be a part of Guided Reading—often providing the easier reading half of the grade-level and easier reading we try to provide each week. **Other books, not big and not predictable, are read by the class or a small flexible group.** These books might be part of a basal series or they might be multiple copies of tradebooks. **The emphasis shifts from read together to reading with partners or on your own.** Instead of reading the selection first to the children, as basals often suggest and teachers often do in first grade, **second-grade teachers should let the children read it first by themselves or with a partner, and problem solve how to figure out new words. Teachers take children on a picture walk through the book leading the children to name the things in the pictures, make predictions, and point out a few critical vocabulary words students might encounter difficulty with as they attempt the reading of the selection. Children then attempt the reading of the selection individually, with a partner or in a small flexible group with the teacher or another helper. The class reconvenes, discusses the selection, and then sometimes reads it in some other whole-class format** (not round-robin reading, however!). **Comprehension strategies are taught and practiced. Predictions made before reading are checked. Story maps and webs are completed.**

The next reading of the selection might include a writing activity. This writing activity is also done by some children individually, some with partners and others in a group guided by an adult. This writing in response to reading is not the Writing Block, however! **Often, the next reading is an acting out of the selection, with various children playing different parts as the rest of the class reads or tells the story.**

Making the *Guided Reading* Block Multilevel

Guided Reading is the hardest block to make multilevel. Any selection is going to be too hard for some children and too easy for others. We don't worry anymore about those children for whom grade-level Guided Reading material is too easy because the other three blocks provide many beyond-grade level opportunities. In addition, our end-of-year results always indicate that students who begin second grade with high literacy levels read well above grade-level.

We do, however, worry about those students for whom grade-level selections are too hard. To make this block meet the needs of children who read below grade level, teachers make a variety of adaptations. **Guided reading time is not spent in grade-level material all week. Rather, teachers choose two selections—one grade-level and one easier—to read each week. Each selection is read several times, each time for a different purpose in a different format.** Rereading enables children who couldn't read it fluently the first time to achieve fluent reading by the last reading. **Children who need help are not left to read by themselves but are supported in a variety of ways. Most teachers use reading partners and teach children how to help their partners rather than do all their** reading for them. While some children read the selection by themselves and others read with partners, **teachers usually meet with small groups of children. These teacher-supported small groups change on a daily basis and do not include only the low readers.**

In addition to the daily Guided Reading Block in which all children are included, **many teachers schedule a 10 minute easy reading support group in which very easy books are read and reread. This group of five to six children changes daily. All children are included at least one day each week.** Children who need easy reading are included more often but not every day. One way or another, we try to assure that every child has some Guided Reading instruction in material at instructional level or easier several days each week. (For other ways to manage the various levels of children during Guided Reading, see Cunningham & Allington, 1994.)

SELF-SELECTED READING

Historically called individualized reading or personalized reading (Veatch,1959), many teachers now label their Self-Selected Reading time "Reader's Workshop" (Routman, 1995). Regardless of what it is called, **Self-Selected Reading is that part of a balanced literacy program when children get to choose what they want to read and what parts of their reading they want to respond to.** Opportunities are provided for children to share and respond to what is read. **Teachers hold individual conferences with children about their books.**

In our classrooms, the Self-Selected Reading Block includes (and usually begins with) teacher read-aloud. The teacher reads to the children from a wide range of literature. Next, children read "on their own level" from a variety of books. In some classrooms, the children read at their desks from crates of books which rotate from table to table. Each crate contains a wide range of levels and types of books, and children choose books from that crate. In other classrooms, you will see children reading at a variety of places. In addition to a reading center, many classrooms have a big book center, a magazine center, a class-authored book center, a science center which includes informational books on the current science topic, a center full of books by a particular author being studied, a taped-book listening center, and sometimes even a computer center with a book on CD. **At Self-Selected Reading time, children go to these centers. In some classrooms, they rotate through the centers on different days, and in other classrooms they choose which center they want to go to.**

Regardless of where the children are, classrooms with successful Self-Selected Reading time all rigorously enforce the "No Wandering" rule. Once you get to your spot, you stay there!

A commonly-observed phenomenon in homes where four-year olds have books and someone to read those books to them is what we call pretend reading. Young children want to do all the things the big people can do. They pretend to cook, to drive, to be the mommy or the daddy, and they pretend they can read. **They do this pretend reading to a younger child or to a stuffed animal, and they do it with a book which they have insisted on having read to them over and over until they can "read" the book! (In fact, this insistence on having a favorite book read hundreds of times is probably motivated by their desire to learn to read!)**

Another way young children read books is by reading the pictures. This is usually done with an informational picture book on a topic of great interest to the child. The parent and the child have probably looked at "the airplane book" or "the dinosaurs book" hundreds of times, spending more time talking about the pictures than actually reading the words. In fact, some of these books have wonderful pictures and lots of sophisticated text, and parents don't read the text at all; they just lead the child to talk about the pictures.

We teach our early first graders that there are three ways to read. A few second-grade students need this information at the beginning of the year if they are to read independently. We tell them they can **"pretend read"** by telling the story of a familiar story book. You can **"picture read"** by looking at a book about real things with lots of pictures and talking about all the things you see in the

pictures. And **you can read by reading all the words.** Early in the year, we model all types of reading and look at books and decide how children at their age would probably read the book.

> "The Gingerbread Man is a book you could pretend read because you know the story so well. Let's practice how you might pretend read it if you choose it for Self-Selected Reading time."

> "How would you read this book about trucks? It's got lots and lots of words in little tiny print, but you could read it by picture reading. Let's practice picture reading."

> "Now, here is an alphabet book. You see just one word and it goes with the picture. You can probably read this book by reading the words."

Once children know that there are three ways to read books, no child ever says, "I can't read yet!"

While the children read, the teacher holds individual conferences with children. Most teachers designate the children as Monday, Tuesday, Wednesday, etc., and then conference with them on their day, spending three or four minutes with each child. Children know that on their day, they should bring one book which they have selected to share with the teacher. They read (in whichever of the three ways is appropriate for that book) a few pages to the teacher and discuss the book and why they chose it. Thus, each child gets a short but dependable conference time with the teacher each week to share what they like about books.

136

Making the *Self-Selected Reading Block* Multilevel

Self-Selected Reading is, by definition, multilevel. The component of Self-Selected Reading that makes it multilevel is the fact that children choose what they want to read. These choices, however, can be limited by what reading materials are available and how willing and able children are to read from the available resources. Fielding and Roller (1992) sum up the problem many struggling readers have with Self-Selected Reading:

> While most of the children are quiet, engaged, and reading during independent reading times, there are always a few children who are not. They are picking up spilled crayons, sweeping up shavings from the pencil sharpener, making trips to the water fountain, walking back and forth alongside bookcases, opening and closing books, and gazing at pictures (p. 678).

The article goes on to indicate that many of the children who "wander round" during Self-Selected Reading time are the ones whose reading ability is limited. The article concludes that:

> Either they do not know how to find a book that they can read, or there is no book available that they can read, or they do not want to read the books they can read. These children remind us of Groucho Marx. They refuse to become a member of any club that will accept them. In book terms, they cannot read the books they want to read, and they do not want to read the books they can read (p. 679).

Fielding and Roller go on to make excellent and practical suggestions about how to support children in reading books they want to read which, without support, would be too difficult and how to make the reading of easy books both enjoyable and socially acceptable. These suggestions include:

- **helping children determine when a book is just right**

- **encouraging children to read books which the teacher has read aloud**

- **encouraging children to read with a friend and to do repeated readings of books they enjoy**

- **teacher modeling the enjoyment to be found in easier books**

- **setting up programs in which children read to younger children and thus have a real purpose for engaging easy books**

- **making lots of informational picture books available.**

Although they do not use the term, following their suggestions would make the Self-Selected Reading time more multilevel. We have incorporated many of their ideas in our Self-Selected Reading Block, and, in addition, we steer our more advanced readers toward books that challenge them.

WRITING

The Writing Block is carried out in "Writers' Workshop" fashion (Graves, 1995; Routman, 1995; Calkins, 1998). It begins with a 10-minute mini-lesson. The teacher sits at the overhead projector or with a large piece of chart paper. The teacher writes and models all the things writers do (although not all on any one day!). The teacher thinks aloud—deciding what to write about and then writes. While writing, the teacher models looking at the *Word Wall* for a troublesome word which is there as well as inventing the spelling of a few big words. The teacher also makes a few mistakes relating to the items currently on the editor's checklist. When the piece is finished or during the following day's mini-lesson, the children help the teacher edit the piece for the items on the checklist. Next the children go to their own writing. They are at all different stages of the writing process—finishing a story, starting a new story, editing, illustrating, etc. While the children write, the teacher conferences with individuals who are getting ready to publish. From 3-5 pieces, they choose one to make into a book. This piece is edited with the teacher's help and the child proceeds to the publishing table where he or she will copy the edited piece and finally illustrate the book. This block ends with "author's chair" in which several students each day share work in progress or their published book with the class.

Early in second grade, our Writing Block begins with what we call the half and half stage. The teacher uses a paper that is half lined, and the other half is used for the picture. Drawing a picture helps some children to visualize and, therefore, write better.

For the mini-lesson, the teacher writes on a large sheet of chart paper or on an overhead transparency. She thinks aloud and writes her sentences, telling the children what she is doing and why. Sometimes she does a shared writing with the children letting them suggest sentences and tell her how to write them.

Next, the children do their writing, and (if you have timed the move correctly) most children write a few sentences. The teacher goes around and encourages and, if asked to spell a word, does not spell, but rather helps the child stretch the word out and get down some letters. After 15-20 minutes, the children gather together, and some children share their pieces. The teacher responds positively to what they tell, including to those few children who only have a picture! The next move is from the half-and-half stage to the stage in which children are writing on their own without teacher encouragement/ stretching out words. The teacher can now spend the 15-20 minutes when the children are writing to help children revise, edit, and publish pieces. This is also the time when we begin to use the author's chair procedure in which the Monday children share on Monday one piece they have written since last Monday, the Tuesday children on Tuesday, etc.

Making the *Writing Block* Multilevel

Writing is the most multilevel block because it is not limited by the availability or acceptability of appropriate books. If teachers allow children to choose their own topics, accept whatever level of first-draft writing each child can accomplish, and allow them to work on their pieces as many days as needed, all children can succeed in writing. One of the major tenets of process writing is that children should choose their own topic. When children decide what they will write about, they write about something of particular interest to them and consequently something that they know about. Now this may seem like belaboring the obvious, but it is a crucial component in making process writing multilevel. When everyone writes about the same topic, the different levels of children's knowledge and writing ability become painfully obvious.

In one of our classrooms, recently, two boys followed each other in the Author's Chair. Todd, a very advanced writer, read a book he had authored titled *Rocks*. His 16 page-book contained illustrations and detailed descriptions of metamorphic, igneous, and sedimentary rocks. The next author was Joey, one of the struggling readers and writers in the classroom. He proudly read his eight-page illustrated book titled *My New Bike*. Listening to the two boys read, the difference in their literacy level was striking. Later, several of the children were individually asked what they liked about the two pieces and how they were different. The children replied that "Todd wrote about rocks and Joey wrote about his bike." Opinions about the pieces were divided, but most children seemed to prefer the bike piece to the rock piece—bikes being of greater interest than rocks to most young children!

In addition to teacher acceptance, children choosing their own topics, and not expecting finished pieces each day, Writer's Workshops include two teaching opportunities which promote the multilevelness of process writing—mini-lessons and publishing conferences. In mini-lessons, the teacher writes and the children get to watch her thinking. In these daily short lessons, teachers show all aspects of the writing process. They model topic selection, planning, writing, revising and editing, and they write on a variety of topics in a variety of different forms.

Some days they write short pieces. Other days, they begin a piece that takes several days to complete. When doing a longer piece, they model how you reread what you wrote previously in order to pick up your train of thought and continue writing. The mini-lesson contributes to making process writing multilevel when the teacher includes all different facets of the writing process, writes on a variety of topics in a variety of forms, and intentionally writes some shorter easier pieces and some more involved longer pieces.

Another opportunity for meeting the various needs and levels of children comes in the publishing conference. In some classrooms as children develop in their writing, children do some peer revising/editing and then come to the teacher "editor-in-chief" for some final revision/editing before publishing. As teachers help children publish the piece they have chosen, they have the opportunity to truly "individualize" their teaching. Looking at the writing of the child usually reveals both what the child needs to move forward and what the child is ready to understand. The editing conference provides the "teachable moment" in which both advanced and struggling writers can be nudged forward in their literacy development.

Finally, writing is multilevel because for some children writing is their best avenue to becoming readers. Decades ago, Russell Stauffer (1970) advocated language experience as an approach to teaching reading in which children found success because they could both read their own words (language) and comprehend their own experiences. When children who are struggling with reading write about their own experiences and then read it back (even if no one else can read it!), they are using their own language and experiences to become readers. Often these children who struggle with even the simplest material during Guided Reading can read everything in their writing notebook or folder. **When children are writing, some children are really working on becoming better writers; others are engaging in the same activity, but for them, writing is how they figure out reading.**

WORKING WITH WORDS

In the Working with Words Block—which is the focus of this book, children learn to read and spell high-frequency words and learn the patterns which allow them to decode and spell lots of words. The first ten minutes of this block are usually given to reviewing the *Word Wall* words. The remaining 15-25 minutes of words time is given to an activity which helps children learn to decode and spell. A variety of different activities are used on different days. Five popular activities are: *Rounding up the Rhymes, Making Words, Guess the Covered Word, Reading/Writing Rhymes*, and *Using Words You Know*. These activities are explained each month in the preceding pages of this book.

Making the *Words Block* Multilevel

Throughout this book, we have described how the words activities are multilevel.

CONNECTIONS ACROSS THE BLOCKS

So far, we have been describing the blocks as separate entities. In most primary classrooms, they each have their allotted time, and you can tell when you watch which block the teacher and children are in. **As much as possible, teachers try to make connections from one block to another.** Many teachers take a theme-approach to teaching. These teachers often select books for Guided Reading which correlate with their theme. During the writing mini-lesson when the teacher models writing, he often (but not every day) writes something connected to the theme. Some of the books teachers read aloud at the beginning of Self-Selected Reading and some of the books children can choose from are theme connected.

Theme words are not put on the *Word Wall*— which we reserve for high-frequency words and words that represent high-frequency patterns. But, most teachers have a theme board or chart in addition to the *Word Wall*. This board changes with each theme and, in addition to pictures, includes theme-related words which children will need as they pursue that theme. Often the secret word in a *Making Words* lesson is theme connected. Sometimes, the sentences a teacher writes for a *Guess the Covered Word* lesson relate to the theme.

In addition to theme connections, there are other connections across the blocks. We practice *Word Wall* words during the words block but we select them once they have been introduced in Guided Reading, and we make sure that the children know that when they are writing, they spell words as best they can unless the word is on the *Word Wall*. *Word Wall* words must be spelled correctly!

Rounding up the Rhymes occurs during the words block, but the book from which we are rounding has usually been read by the children during Guided Reading or read-aloud by the teacher to begin the Self-Selected Reading Block. Sometimes, we do *Guess the Covered Word* activities by using self-adhesive notes to cover one word on each page of a big book. We often introduce vocabulary during Guided Reading through picture walks, and, while reading with small groups, we coach children on how to decode words using picture, context, and letter sound clues.

In our mini-lesson at the beginning of each day's writing time, we model how we can find words we need on the *Word Wall* and how to stretch out words listening for the sounds to spell big words not available in the room. When we are helping children edit, we praise them for their good attempts and spelling and coach them to use things they are learning during the Words Block.

Most teachers who have organized their framework within the Four-Blocks Framework find that it is natural and easy to make connections across the blocks. By providing instruction in all four blocks, we provide children with many different ways to learn to read and write. **Connections across the blocks help children build bridges between what they are learning.**

ASSESSMENT AND EVALUATION

In the last several years, several schools and districts have attempted to evaluate the effectiveness of the Four-Blocks Framework. We will report some data from three different sites.

Data from the Original Four-Blocks School

Clemmons Elementary School, the school in which the framework was originally implemented, is a large suburban school with a diverse student population. Some children come from homes surrounding the school, and others are bussed from the inner city. In any year, 20-25% of children qualify for free or reduced-priced lunches. Approximately 25-30% of the children are African-American, Hispanic, Asian, or Pacific Islander. Since the program began, the student population has remained relatively stable, with approximately 10% of the children moving in and out each year. There have been three different administrators. Approximately half of the current first- and second-grade teachers have been there for all six years. All classes are heterogeneously grouped. No children are retained and children are not referred for special classes until second grade. Thus, the population of this study includes all children who are in the school at the end of first and second grade. The majority of the children have had two years of multi-method, multilevel instruction, but some children who are new to the school have had a year or less.

Throughout the year, teachers conduct assessment by observing and conferencing with children, taking Running Records and looking at writing samples. At the end of the year, children are given the Basic Reading Inventory (Johns, 1994). Instructional levels on the oral reading passages are computed using the standard procedures. Because the IRI is administered at the end of the year, an instructional level of first or second grade is considered grade level at the end of first grade and an instructional level of second or third grade is considered grade level at the end of second grade.

IRI Data is reported starting with our second year in which all first-grade teachers were involved and continues through five years of first graders and second graders. Approximately 100-140 children in each grade are included in each year's data.

Eight years of multimethod, multilevel instruction

Year 1 (Pilot study in *one* first-grade classroom) 1989 – 1990

Year 2 (Grade 1)	1991			Year 3 (Grade 2)	1992	
Reading levels:	No.	Percentage		Reading levels:	No.	Percentage
Above (Grades 3 – 6)	64	63%		Above (Grades 4 – 6)	77	75%
At (Grades 1 – 2)	28	27%		At (Grades 2 – 3)	24	23%
Below (PP, P)	10	10%		Below (PP, P, Grade 1)	2	2%

Year 3 (Grade 1)	1992			Year 4 (Grade 2)	1993	
Reading levels:	No.	Percentage		Reading levels:	No.	Percentage
Above (Grades 3 – 6)	65	62%		Above (Grades 4 – 6)	74	71%
At (Grades 1 – 2)	26	25%		At (Grades 2 – 3)	21	20%
Below (PP, P)	14	13%		Below (PP, P, Grade 1)	9	9%

Year 4 (Grade 1)	1993			Year 5 (Grade 2)	1994	
Reading levels:	No.	Percentage		Reading levels:	No.	Percentage
Above (Grades 3 – 6)	76	61%		Above (Grades 4 – 6)	87	68%
At (Grades 1 – 2)	28	22%		At (Grades 2 – 3)	32	25%
Below (PP, P)	21	17%		Below (PP, P, Grade 1)	9	7%

Year 5 (Grade 1)	1994			Year 6 (Grade 2)	1995	
Reading levels:	No.	Percentage		Reading levels:	No.	Percentage
Above (Grades 3 – 6)	59	58%		Above (Grades 4 – 6)	76	78%
At (Grades 1 – 2)	25	25%		At (Grades 2 – 3)	16	16%
Below (PP, P)	17	17%		Below (PP, P, Grade 1)	6	6%

Year 6 (Grade 1)	1995			Year 7 (Grade 2)	1996	
Reading levels:	No.	Percentage		Reading levels:	No.	Percentage
Above (Grades 3 – 6)	87	64%		Above (Grades 4 – 6)	97	70%
At (Grades 1 – 2)	29	22%		At (Grades 2 – 3)	31	22%
Below (PP, P)	19	14%		Below (PP, P, Grade 1)	10	8%

Year 7 (Grade 1)	1996			Year 8 (Grade 2)	1997	
Reading levels:	No.	Percentage		Reading levels:	No.	Percentage
Above (Grades 3 – 6)	85	64%		Above (Grades 4 – 6)	118	74%
At (Grades 1 – 2)	32	24%		At (Grades 2 – 3)	26	20%
Below (PP, P)	15	11%		Below (PP, P, Grade 1)	8	6%

Across the eight years, instructional level results have remained remarkably consistent. At the end of first grade, 58-64% of the children read above grade level—third grade or above; 22-28% read on grade level; 10-17% read below grade level—preprimer or primer. On average, one child each year is unable to meet the instructional level criteria on the preprimer passage. At the end of second grade, the number at grade level is 14-25%. The number above grade level—fourth grade level or above—increases to 68-76%. The number reading below grade level drops to 2-9%, half what it was in first grade (*The Reading Teacher*, Vol. 51, No. 8, May 1998, 652-664).

While we have no control group to which we can compare our results, our data was collected across eight years and was consistent across five groups of 100-140 children. The data looks remarkably similar even though half the teachers have come since the onset, and the school has had several changes in administration. Looking at this data across eight years, the most startling (and encouraging) results relate to those children who do not read at grade level at the end of first grade. Out of 100 plus children each year, approximately one child is unable to read the IRI preprimer passage. This child should not be considered a nonreader, however, because this child does have simple predictable books he or she can read and can also read his/her own writing!

Of the 10-15 percent of children who do not read at grade level at the end of first grade, half are reading on or, in some cases, above grade level at the end of second grade. Looking at the first-grade data, it is impossible to predict which children will make the leap. Some children who read at the preprimer level at the end of first grade read at grade level or above at the end of second grade. Others who read further along—primer level—at the end of first grade only move to first reader level by the end of second grade.

Standardized test data on these children collected in third, fourth, and fifth grades each year indicates that 90% of the children are in the top two quartiles. Most years, we have no children whose scores fall in the bottom quartile.

Data from a suburban school district

The original school in which the framework was implemented does not do standardized testing until the end of third grade. Thus, we had to rely on our IRI data to assess the progress of our students. While we feel that IRI data is the best indicator of individual growth in reading, standardized tests have established reliability and are not subject to individual tester bias/skill as IRI's are. We considered the idea of administering standardized tests to all our first and second graders but rejected this notion because of the time and money involved and because we would have no comparable control group. Meanwhile, other districts heard about, visited, and implemented the framework. Many of these districts did administer standardized reading tests in the primary grades, and one district devised an evaluation model, the results of which will be reported here.

Lexington One in Lexington, South Carolina is a suburban southeastern school district with eight elementary schools, in which 25% of the children qualify for free/reduced price lunch. During the 1995-96 school year, first-grade teachers in the district were given information about the Four-Blocks Framework and allowed to choose whether or not they wanted to implement the framework in their classrooms. Approximately half of the teachers chose to implement the framework and were provided with several workshops/ books and collegial support throughout the year in their classrooms.

In January 1996, 100 first graders in classrooms using the Four-Blocks Framework and 100 first graders in classrooms not using the framework were randomly selected and were given the Word Recognition in Isolation and Word Recognition in Context sections of the Basic Reading Inventory (Johns, 1994). Adjusted means for both measures favored students in the Four-Blocks classrooms. For the word recognition in context means, the differences were statistically significant. Students in the Four-Blocks classrooms were on average reading at the beginning of second-grade level. Students in the other first grades were on average at the first grade, second month level.

While these results were encouraging, district officials were concerned about lack of reliability on the IRI and about teacher bias, fearing that the enthusiasm of the teachers who chose to implement the model may have created a Hawthorne effect. They then devised an experiment using cohort analysis and standardized test results. In May of 1996, all 557 first graders in Four-Blocks classrooms were administered the Metropolitan Achievement Test. Each child was matched with a first grader from the previous year (1994-95) based on their scores on the CSAB (Cognitive Skills Assessment Battery), a test of readiness given each year during the first week of school. The total reading mean score for the Four-Blocks first graders was significantly better (.0001 level) than that of the previous years matched students. In grade equivalent terms, the average Four-Blocks first grader's total reading was 2.0 while that of the 1994-95 student was 1.6.

Based on the standardized test data, school officials concluded that the Four-Blocks Framework had been much more effective than their previous ability-grouped traditional basal instruction. They hypothesized that since students selected for the cohort group had been taught by all the first-grade teachers in the system, teacher bias based on the enthusiasm of teachers choosing to change could not have accounted for the results. Furthermore, their classroom observations suggested that teachers who implemented the Four-Blocks Framework had not all implemented it fully or equally well. In spite of the unequal implementation, with all children in Four-Blocks classrooms included, they scored on average almost half a year better than the previous group.

This district then analyzed their data by dividing both groups of students into thirds according to their CSAB scores. Figure 1 demonstrates graphically that children of all ability levels profited from the multilevel Four-Block instruction. There was a 15 point difference in total reading scores for the lower third, a 23 point difference for the middle third, and a 28 point difference for the upper third. The district concluded that organizing in this nonability grouped way had profited the struggling students and had been even more successful for students who would traditionally have been placed in the top group (*Reading Teacher*, 662).

**Lexington School District
Four-Blocks Program vs. Controls
MAT-7 total reading score**

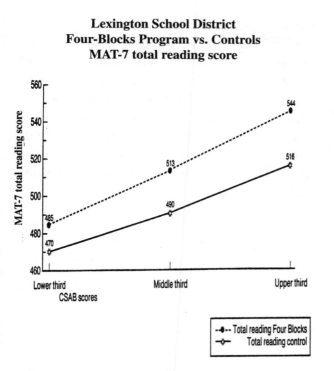

During the 1993-94 school year, another new superintendent arrived. The district continued to emphasize whole language and teachers were trained in cooperative learning. This year's test scores showed some improvement at grades two and three, though none at grade one. During the 1994-95 school year, teachers were urged to continue to use whole language and cooperative learning, and they were also trained in the Learning Styles approach of Rita Dunn. It is hard to compare test scores for this year because the state changed from the Stanford Achievement Test to the Metropolitan Achievement Test, but scores were the worst they had ever been. In grade one, only 20% of the students scored at or above the 50th percentile on total reading. At the second-grade level, only 9% scored at or above the 50th percentile.

During the 1995-96 school year, all ten teachers—six at first grade and four at second grade—were trained in and mandated to try the Four-Blocks Framework. (It boggles the mind to imagine how enthusiastic and confident these teachers must have been to implement one more "miracle solution!"). These teachers were given workshops/books, state-department, central office support, etc., and in the opinion of those central office and state department facilitators who visited weekly in their classrooms, four of the six first-grade teachers and three of the four second-grade teachers implemented the framework.

MAT total reading scores for all first and second graders in that school (including the three classes which did not really implement the framework) indicated that 30% of the first graders and 38% of the second graders had total reading scores at or above the 50th percentile.

Data from One Rural School

During the same year, a nearby school adopted the Four-Blocks Framework and mandated its use in all first- and second-grade classrooms. Brockington Elementary School in Florence School District Four in Timmonsville, South Carolina is a small rural district in which 84% of students qualify for free/reduced price lunch. Based on low achievement tests scores, the elementary school had been placed on the list of schools with lowest scores and had tried a variety of approaches to improving reading and math test scores. During the 1991-92 school year, the school was mandated by a new superintendent to "teach the basics." A state-developed basic skills curriculum focused on "skill and drill" was implemented along with a computer-lab basic skills remediation program for Chapter 1 students. End of the year achievement test scores showed no improvement. During the 1992-93 school year, teachers took a year-long graduate course on whole language. Again, the end-of-year test results failed to show improvement.

The data from this school system are, of course, open to interpretation. Since different children were tested in the 1994-95 group and we have no pretest data on these children, we cannot be sure that the huge jump in the number of children reading at or above grade level is due to the implementation of the Four-Blocks Framework. Officials in this school district, having tried literally "almost everything" in the previous five years, are convinced, however, that the differences are real and attributable to the balanced multilevel instruction which most of the 1995-96 first and second graders received on a daily basis. They continue the implementation the next year and the results of the end-of-year testing can be seen on the following chart.

The last eight years have been exciting and satisfying years for us. We have seen the Four-Blocks Framework implemented in hundreds of classrooms in diverse settings, with varied populations of children. This framework has few revolutionary ideas but it provides teachers with a way to implement a balanced program and more nearly meet the needs of children with a wide range of levels who do not all learn in the same way.

**MAT 7 Norm Referenced Test
Comparison of Percentage of Students
Scoring at Each Quarter**

GRADE 2 DATA	Reading		
Percentile	1995	1996	1997
76-100%	1	14	11
51-75%	5	20	27
26-50%	25	40	38
1-25%	68	26	24

Concepts of Print Checklist	• Starts on left.	• Goes left to right.	• Makes return sweep to next line.	• Matches words by pointing to each as reading.	• Can point to just one word.	• Can point to the first word and the last word.	• Can point to just one letter.	• Can point to the first letter and the last letter.

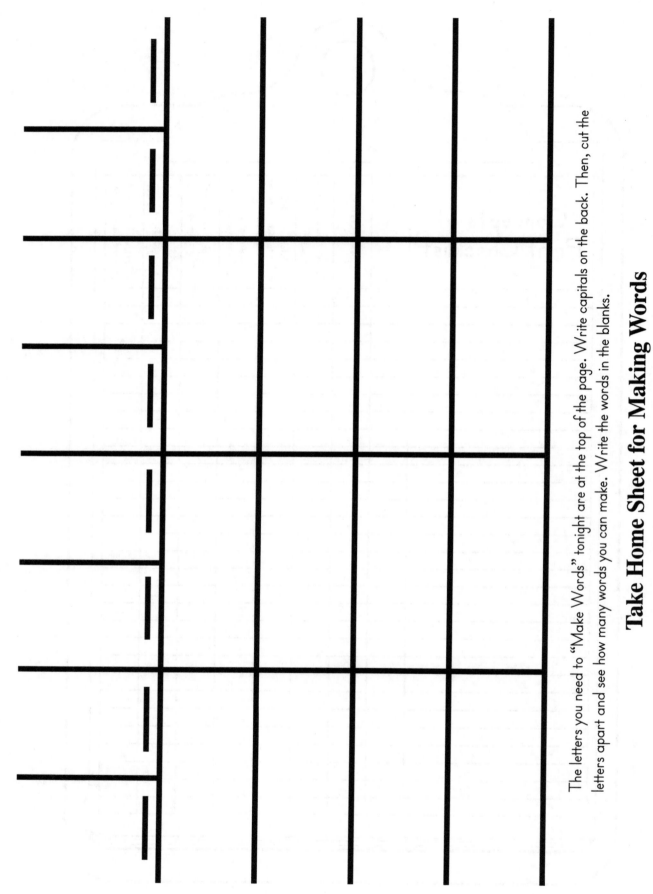

The letters you need to "Make Words" tonight are at the top of the page. Write capitals on the back. Then, cut the letters apart and see how many words you can make. Write the words in the blanks.

Take Home Sheet for Making Words

I'm Using
What I Know
When I'm Reading

**I'm Using
What I Know
When I'm Writing**

150

Directions for a Picture Dictionary (see page 14)

The list on page 15 shows beginning sounds appropriate for second grade. Three different reproducibles can be found on pages 152-154.

The letters **a, e, h, i, j, k, l, m, n, o, q, r, u, v, w, x, y,** and **z** used a page with one letter box. Start the page by having students write the letter in both upper- and lowercase in the box. Next, discuss words that begin with this letter. Page 15 will help you. Any word students mention that begins with the letter can be used on that page. Students can choose two or three words to illustrate and spell on the top of each page. They need to leave space as the picture dictionary should grow with them throughout the year as they continue to read and write.

With letters like **b, f, p,** and **t,** you will need a single page for words that begin with these consonants and a double page for words that begin with consonant clusters like **bl/br, fl/fr, pl/pr,** and **th/tr**.

For **c,** you will need a double page for the two sounds **c(k)** and **c(s)** and a triple page for **ch, cl,** and **cr** words.

For **d,** you could use two single pages or a double page for the **d** and **dr** words.

For **g,** you would use a single sheet for **g** and a triple for words that begin with **gl, gr,** and **g(j)**.

For **s,** you would use a double for **s** and **sh,** and three triples for **sc/sk/sl, sm/sn/sp, st/str/sw** words.

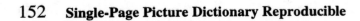

Single-Page Picture Dictionary Reproducible

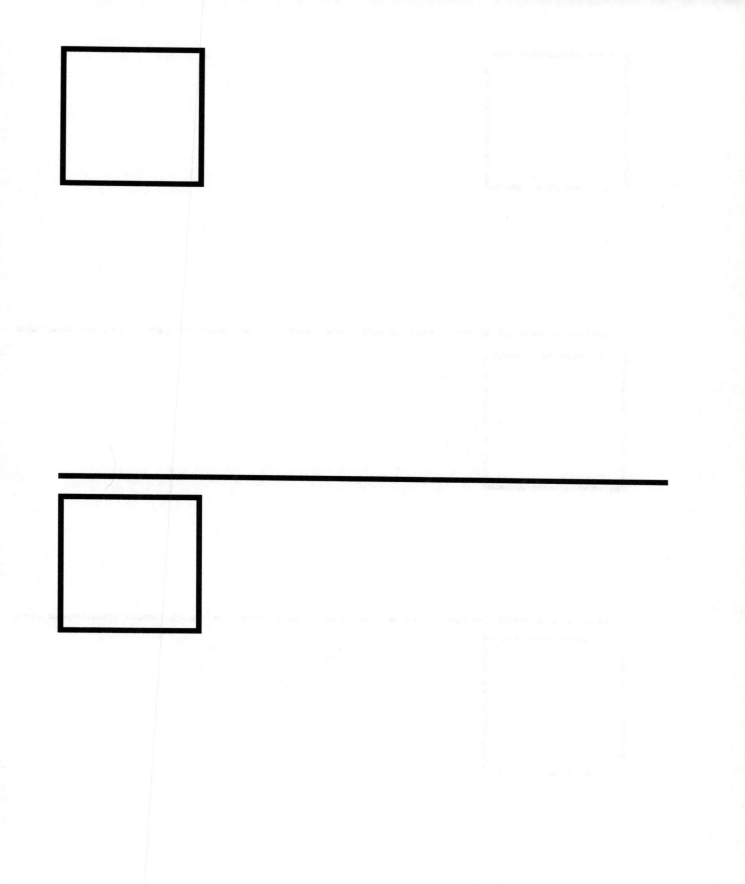

Double-Page Picture Dictionary Reproducible 153

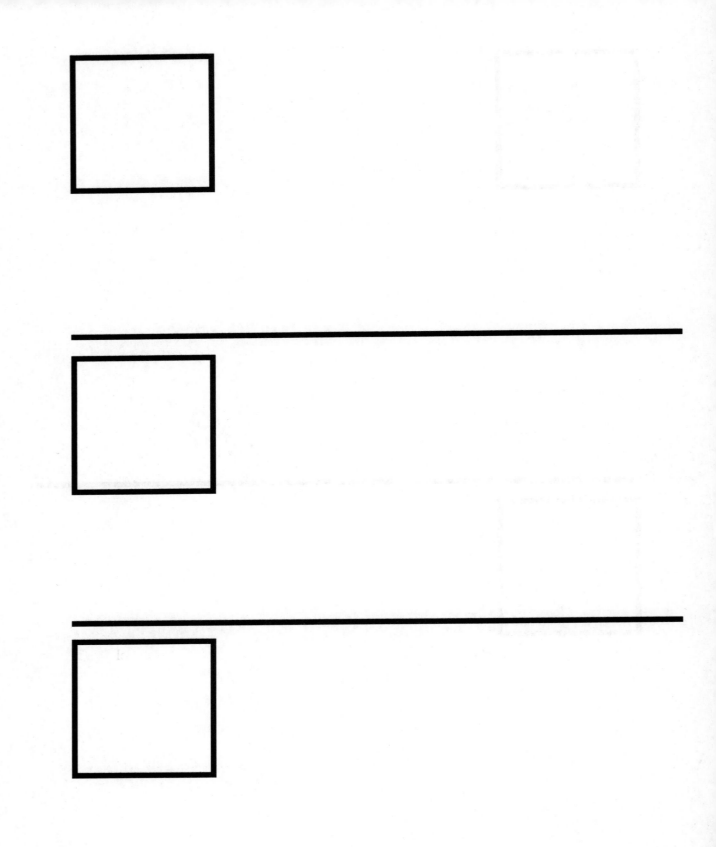

Triple-Page Picture Dictionary Reproducible

REFERENCES

PROFESSIONAL CITATIONS

Adams, M.J. *Beginning to Read: Thinking and Learning About Print*. Cambridge, MA: MIT Press, 1990.

Allington, R. L. "The Reading Instruction Provided Readers of Differing Reading Ability." *Elementary School Journal*, 83, (1983) 549-559.

Allington, R. L. (1991). "Effective Literacy Instruction for At-Risk Children." In *Better schooling for the children of poverty: Alternatives to conventional wisdom* edited by M. Knapp & P. Shields(Eds.), 9-30. Berkeley, CA: McCutchan, 1991.

Bond, G. L., & Dykstra, R. "The Cooperative Research Program in First Grade Reading Instruction." *Reading Research Quarterly*, 2, (1967): 5-142.

Calkins, L. M. (1994). *The Art of Teaching Writing*. (2nd. ed.). Portsmouth, NH: Heinemann, 1994.

Clay, M. *An Observation Survey of Early Literacy Achievement*. Portsmouth, NH: Heinemann, 1993.

Cunningham, P.M. *Phonics They Use: Words for Reading and Writing*. (2nd. ed.). New York: HarperCollins, 1995.

Cunningham, P. M. & Hall, D. P. *The Four Blocks: A Framework for Reading and Writing in Classrooms That Work*. 1995. This video is available from I.E.S.S. by calling 800-644-5280.

Cunningham, P. M. & Hall, D. P. *Making Words*, Carthage, IL: Good Apple, 1994.

Cunningham, P. M. & Hall, D. P. *Making More Words*, Carthage, IL: Good Apple, 1997.

Cunningham, P. M. & Allington, R. L. *Classrooms That Work: They Can All Read and Write*. New York: HarperCollins, 1994.

Cunningham, P. M. & Cunningham, J. W. "Making Words: Enhancing the Invented Spelling-Decoding Connection." *The Reading Teacher*, 46, (1992): 106-115.

Cunningham, P. M., Hall, D. P. & Defee, M. "Nonability Grouped, Multilevel Instruction: A Year in a First Grade Classroom." *Reading Teacher*, 44, (1991): 566-571.

Cunningham, P. M., Hall, D. P. & Defee, M. "Nonability Grouped, Multilevel Instruction: Eight Years Later." *Reading Teacher*, 51, (1998).

Cunningham, P. M., Hall, D. P., & Sigmon, C.M. *The Teacher's Guide to The Four Blocks*. Greensboro, NC: Carson-Dellosa Publishing, 1998.

Cunningham, P. M., Hall, D. P., & Kohfeldt, J. "Word Wall Plus for Second Grade." Greensboro, NC: Carson-Dellosa Publishing, 1998.

Fielding, L. & Roller, C. "Making Difficult Books Accessible and Easy Books Acceptable." *The Reading Teacher*, 45, (1992): 678-685.

Gentry, J.R. *Spel. . .is a Four Letter Word.* Portsmouth, NH: Heinemann, 1987.

Gentry, J.R. & Gillet, J.W. *A Fresh Look at Spelling.* Portsmouth, NH: Heineman, 1994.

Graves, D. H. *A Fresh Look at Writing.* Portsmouth, NH. Heinemann, 1995.

Hall, D. P., Prevatte, C. & Cunningham, P. M. "Eliminating Ability Grouping and Reducing Failure in the Primary Grades." In *No Quick Fix* edited by Allington, R. L and Walmsley, S. (Eds.), 137-158. Teachers College Press, 1995.

Johns, J. L. *Basic Reading Inventory.* (5th ed.) Dubuque, IA: Kendall Hunt, 1994.

Mullis, I. V. S., & Jenkins, L. B. *The Reading Report Card. 1971-88.* Washington, DC: U. S. Department of Education, 1990.

Routman, R. *Invitations.* Portsmouth, NH: Heinemann, 1994.

Shepard, L. A., & Smith, M. L. "Synthesis of Research on Grade Retention." *Educational Leadership*, 47, (1990): 84-88.

Sigmon, Cheryl Mahaffey. *Implementing the Four-Block Literacy Model.* Greensboro, NC: Carson-Dellosa Publishing, 1997.

Stauffer, R. G. *The Language-Experience Approach to the Teaching of Reading.* New York: Harper Row, 1970.

Veatch, J. *Individualizing Your Reading Program; Self-Selection in Action.* NY: Putnam, 1959.

CHILDREN'S BOOKS CITED:

All Aboard ABC, by Doug Magee & Robert Newman. (Puffin Unicorn Books, 1990).

A My Name is Alice, by Jane Bayer. (Dial Books, 1990).

Animalia, by Graeme Base. (Puffin Books, 1996).

Annie, Bea, and Chi Chi Delores: A School Day Alphabet, by Donna Maurer. (Houghton Mifflin, 1996).

Basketball ABC: The NBA Alphabet, by Florence Cassen Mayer. (Harry N. Abrams, Inc.,1996).

*By the Sea: An Alphabet Book, b*y Ann Blades. (Kids Can Press, 1985).

A Fly in the Sky, by Kristin Pratt. (Dawn Publishing, 1996).

From Apple to Zipper, by Nora Cohen. (Aladdin Books, 1993).

From Letter to Letter, by Terri Sloat. (Puffin Unicorn Books, 1989).

Golden Bear, by Ruth Young. (Scholastic, 1992).

House Mouse, Senate Mouse, by Peter & Cheryl Barnes. (Rosebud Books, 1996).

How I Spent My Summer Vacation, by Mark Teague. (Crown Publishers, 1995).

A Jewish Holiday ABC, by Malka Drucker. (Voyager Books, 1996).

The Monster Book of ABC Sounds, by Alan Snow. (Puffin Pied Piper Books, 1994).

My Nose is a Hose, by Kent Salisbury. (McClanahan,1997).

My Teacher My Friend, by P.K. Hallinan. (Children's Press, 1989).

NBA Action from A to Z, by James Preller. (Scholastic, 1997).

One Fish, Two Fish, Red Fish, Blue Fish, by Dr. Seuss. (Random House, 1960).

One Less Fish, by Kim Michelle Toft & Allan Sheather. (Charlesbridge, 1998).

Puffins Climb, Penguins Rhyme, by Bruce McMillan. (Harcourt Brace, 1995).

Saturday Night at the Dinosaur Stomp, by Carol Diggory Shields. (Scholastic, 1997).

Sea Otters, by Avelyn Davidson. (Shortland Publications, 1998).

Storytellers, by Diana Yurkovic. (Shortland Publications, 1998.)

The Snowy Day, by Ezra Jack Keats. (Puffin Books, 1996).

The Sweet and Sour Alphabet Book, by Langston Hughes. (Oxford University Press, 1997).

This Is the Pumpkin, by Abby Levine. (Albert Whitman & Co., 1997).

This is the Sea That Feeds Us, by Robert Baldwin. (Devon, 1998).

Those Can Do Pigs, by David McPhail. (Scholastic, 1996).

A Walk in the Rainforest, by Kristin Pratt. (Dawn Publishing, 1992).

Woodrow, the White House Mouse, by Peter & Cheryl Barnes. (Rosebud Books, 1995).

Zoo-Looking, by Mem Fox. (Mondo, 1996).